REVELATION AT THE FOOD BANK

ESSAYS

MERRILL JOAN GERBER

Sagging
Meniscus

The essays in *Revelation at the Food Bank* were first published in the following journals:

— "Revelation at the Food Bank": *The Sewanee Review*, Summer 2022
— "True Believer: My Friendship With Cynthia Ozick": *Salmagundi*, Summer 2018
— "Letters Home From College: The Making of a Writer": *The Sewanee Review*, Fall 2017
— "At the DMV": *Salmagundi*, Winter 2016
— "A Life in Letters: A Decades-Long Correspondence With the Italian Writer, Arturo Vivante": *The American Scholar*, Winter 2016
— "The Found Desk": *Salmagundi*, Winter 2013
— "Why I Must Give Up Writing": *The Sewanee Review*, Winter 2007
— "The Harpsichord on the Mountain": *The American Scholar*, Summer 2002
— "The Lost Airman": *Commentary*, 1998
— "On the Edge of the Action: A Conversation With Merrill Joan Gerber by Mario Materassi": *The Sewanee Review*, Summer 1999 (reprinted with permission of Luisa Materassi)

The author thanks Betty Fishman and the Fishman Family Foundation for their support in the publication of this book.

Set in Mrs Eaves with LaTeX.

ISBN: 978-1-952386-70-1 (paperback)
ISBN: 978-1-952386-71-8 (ebook)
Library of Congress Control Number: 2023947560

Sagging Meniscus Press
Montclair, New Jersey
saggingmeniscus.com

for J.S., always

Contents

REVELATION AT THE FOOD BANK

Revelation at the Food Bank

"ID YOU EVER HAVE SEX with another woman?" I asked my husband when he was eighty-five and we had been married for sixty-two years. I could see he was dumbstruck. I was angry about something, maybe about everything, the stupidity of everyone, the mistakes that were made every day by careless, indifferent idiots.

My husband ordered new glasses—just ordinary glasses, a regular pair and a pair of sunglasses—and when the optician's office called to say "Your glasses are ready," he drove ten miles to pick them up only to learn that only one of the two pairs was ready. Was this not ultimate stupidity? Why wouldn't I be angry? My husband rarely gets angry, so I have to be angry for him as well as for myself.

Another time we went to the In-N-Out and ordered two burgers and two fries and extra ketchup. A girl handed me a bag through the window of our car. When we got home, we found she had given us three fries and ketchup, no burgers. Of course, I tried to call when we got home, but you can't call the place where you bought the food—only the corporate offices in some other state. We ate every one of the fries.

I never used to say "fuck." But lately, because our old house is so crowded with fifty years' worth of stuff, things keep falling down on me—books tumble out of bookcases, clothes stream out of closets, and pills crash out of medicine cabinets. Now these cabinets are also full of face masks and latex gloves to be worn while taking in the mail.

At the start of the pandemic, my cleaning lady, who worried about us because we are so old, suggested I go to the food bank because it was safer than going shopping. Why would I go to a food bank when I hadn't lost my job, wasn't homeless, and could pay for my groceries? She insisted that I would be less likely to catch Covid-19. I'd have no contact with people and could stay sealed in my car. She gave me easy directions to the church, told me they were the kindest, nicest folks, and that they gave away free turkeys every Thanksgiving. I so desired a free turkey for once in my life. After our last Thanksgiving, my husband said we should no longer buy a turkey for the holiday—too heavy for him to handle, too hard for him to carve now that he had a tremor, too much leftover food for just two people. Who of our children would even come to have Thanksgiving with us? All our daughters were grown, all lived far away, and not one would be interested in the little chocolate turkeys I used to buy them at See's Candies every Thanksgiving.

I drove the two miles to the food bank at the church—really just one left turn from our street onto the road that goes from our house to the magnificent golden cross at the church's entrance. "Welcome—You Must Wear a Mask" the sign told me, and I joined the orderly line of supplicants winding their way in a colorful parade of cars along a road through the parking lot. Among the cars I noted a BMW, a red Mercedes and a Humvee. A pretty woman at a table greeted each car, one by one. She talked briefly to every driver, and typed something into a small computer. When I got to her, she took my name but didn't ask me if I were poor or homeless, and placed on my windshield a little card that said "ONE SPECIAL ITEM FIRST VISIT."

"Have a great day," she told me, "And God Bless."

When I arrived at a temporary stop sign, an older man bent toward me and asked me kindly, "How many families and where do you want the food? Back seat or trunk?" I told him one family, trunk. He wrote "1-T" on my windshield in white marker. I drove forward and noticed a swarm of volunteers wearing bright orange vests hurrying to the open trunk of the car ahead of me, each person carrying a carton, or a gallon jug of milk, or a bag of vegetables (some celery stalks sticking out the top), or a lumpy foil -wrapped object, shaped, I thought, like a frozen chicken. One woman helper was smiling as she deposited a bag into the car ahead. A young man with powerful muscled arms was loading a large sealed box into the trunk. On its side was printed "LOS ANGELES REGIONAL FOOD BANK" and under it the words: "FIGHTING HUNGER. GIVING HOPE."

My turn now. I stopped, I felt vibrations behind me as my trunk door was raised, and a series of thumps shook my car. The trunk was gently closed; the man wiped the white letters off my windshield, gave me a thumbs up, and I drove off, only to stop at one more station. A woman about my age came to my open car window and said "How can I help you? Baby diapers? Wet wipes? Formula? Hand sanitizer? Masks? Dog food?"

"I don't have a dog." She looked at me closely. "Maxi-pads? At my age I have to use them, maybe you can use some too." Then she astonished me by extending her closed fist through the open window toward me, and I automatically extended mine and we fist-bumped. "Friends!" she announced. She handed me some carefully wrapped portions of maxi-pads. "See you next week, my friend," she said. I drove home, somewhat stunned, aware that I was smiling.

❖

When I opened my trunk in the garage, I felt a rare excitement—a kind of delight that a surprise awaited me, as on a special birthday. I carried a bag of potatoes into the house and asked my husband to help with the rest. The gallon of milk was too heavy for me. The carton, also. We put all the food on the kitchen table.

A beautiful chocolate layer cake, which I guessed was my special first visit item, showed an expiration date two days ago, but I was certain it was perfect. Someone had also placed in my trunk an orchid plant in a red plastic pot. It was mostly wilted, but it still had a few floppy purple flowers hanging off a stem. How kind someone was to do this for me. Even imperfect beauty raised my spirits. In the big carton were bags of rice and beans, a box of spaghetti, cans of tuna, chicken and soup, jars of peanut butter. We unpacked the various bags and found a bottle of cooking oil, a pound of butter, apples, walnuts, carrots, onions. Other gifts I discovered included a can titled "LIQUID DEATH," a bottle of dark truffle ketchup, a six pack of carmel-pumpkin yogurt, and a package of wild sardines in hot jalapeno sauce.

"Do we really need all this?" my husband asked.

"Do we need to eat?" I replied.

❁

Whatever roused my anger toward my husband had been percolating in me for years. He was such a caring and thoughtful man, yet common annoyances surfaced. Why does he put so much cream cheese on his bagel? Or leave lights on in every room of the house? How come he tries to open the front door after our walk before he thinks to put his key in the lock?

At one trip to the food bank, I was given a five-pound bag of frozen diced ham, packaged in a long cylindrical tube. At home, baffled by how to store this inconvenient shape, I'd stuffed it way back in the refrigerator. That night, considering what to cook for dinner, I pulled out the tube. The sealed end split open and five pounds of freezing ham shards shot out and struck my body everywhere, ham juice soaking my pants and running down my legs into my shoes.

"Fuck," I yelled. But wouldn't anyone?

My husband would not. Such words do not abide in him. The anger that comes over me around mealtimes is because I have to make all the meals. We married young, when men were not house-husbands, or cooks, or baby sitters. The man had the job. My husband was a professor, he worked many hours and graded many papers. That was the arrangement. The challenge of every meal belonged to me—three times a day, year after year. I *also* had a job—I wrote stories and books. But *I* did my work at home, where all the other work, including the care of our children, awaited me.

I must have long ago been resourceful and creative about food. I once had a professional deli-meat slicer, a bread-making machine, a blender, a toaster-oven, and a pressure cooker—along with a cake mixer, waffle iron, popcorn popper, tortilla press, and everything you would need to core, peel or shred an apple. Most of those gadgets still crowding my counters and stuffed in my kitchen cabinets have died by now—parts having failed or gone missing, their instruction booklets vanished. I still had one beloved Jewish cook book that contained my favorite banana bread recipe, and I'd written hundreds of dates up and down that single page over the years, the days on which I baked that one perfect bread.

Since I now was stocking up at the food bank, certain foods never showed up at our dinner table. An eggplant, for example. Chicken livers, never. Lox, of course not. Cream cheese, croissants, blintzes, chocolate bars. Whenever I needed something essential, I simply—like everyone else—ordered it from Amazon.

One day my husband said he'd lost his nail clipper so I ordered six of them from Amazon. A big truck came the next day, with a bearded driver in it, to deliver the tiny nail clippers with a key chain attached to each of them.

Another day a soft envelope turned up in my mailbox from Nordstrom, where I never shop. It was addressed to a woman named Linda Black at an address exactly one block to the south of my house. I could feel that whatever was in the envelope was silky and soft, perhaps a nightgown or a blouse. I could imagine it on my very body. Who would ever know if I kept it? I could slit open that package and be the owner of whatever was in it.

However, when my husband saw me bringing in the mail, I told him that a package had been misdelivered. He said we should take a walk and bring it to its rightful owner. I considered telling him I'd do it myself, later. He'd never know I'd kept it. Why is it I've never confided to him the truth about certain lowlife instincts I harbor? Does marriage require these kinds of confessions? Does he conceal such thoughts from me? I doubt he has them. But I often wonder how his truths differ from mine and how much we hide from each other.

We walked to the neighbor's house, rang the bell. The man who lived there opened the door. We didn't know him, though we'd lived in our house over fifty years and passed his house nearly every day on our walks. In truth, we lived in an indifferent and chilly neighborhood.

Taking the package from me, he appeared to recognize, as I had, that the object inside was soft and flexible. He held up a forefinger as if he had just remembered something—and then told us that his wife had died two weeks ago. Of breast cancer. He shook his head sadly at the package. A little dog appeared at his feet as we stood at the door and he bent to pat it gently. Then he thanked us and wished us a good day. Whatever expensive garment had arrived would never be worn, almost certainly would never be returned to the store, and, after all, could have been mine.

Some days later, as we sat outside admiring the oak trees that largely concealed the slope of mountain to the north, we saw the bereaved husband walking his little dog. He waved and was, in fact, coming to our door. He held out to us our bank statement that had been mis-delivered by the mailman to his house. We all agreed heartily that United States postal workers ought to notice that streets have different names even if some of their numbers are the same. *Learn how to read, folks,* I thought.

Now that we seemed to have made a local friend, I was distressed when shortly thereafter, a FOR SALE sign went up in our neighbor's yard. On our next walk, we stopped to pay attention to the garden that he had long ago planted in front of his house—a design of shapely stones, large boulders, and colorful drought- resistant plants. Almost overnight, it seemed, one of those desert-like plants had shot forth a great, phallic stalk skyward. Within days, it sprouted layer upon layer of smaller phallic stalks. With my cell phone I took a picture of the odd creation. An app identified the plant as "Nepenthes" which brings forth growths that look exactly like the human penis. A garden of penises—amazing. Having had only a sister, I never really saw one of them till my wedding night.

The house sold quickly and whoever bought it proceeded to destroy the stone garden and tear out all the beautiful drought-resistant plants. I felt a pang to see those handsome phalluses cut down, but I also realized that the widower's house had a much better view of the mountains than ours. He no doubt sold his house for a lot more money than we would ever get for ours. Thoughts like this convince me that I am unlucky, though my husband tells me often how lucky we are. One of us doesn't see reality clearly.

There are ever-present, recurring reasons to be distressed, to be furious. I seem to contain an automatic switch that, once flipped, destroys whatever state of peace I might briefly achieve. My husband has affectionate advice for me all the time. He takes my hand when he sees me getting agitated, and begs: "Please, just relax." What kind of advice is that? He certainly has experience in relaxing as it is my job to write all the complaint letters, call the banks when they make mistakes, schedule appointments with the tax man, the doctors and dentists, write the checks to the housekeeper and the gardner and the pool guy and notify—when our credit card has to be updated—the twenty places that bill us every month for whatever we endlessly have to pay for.

❁

At the food bank, my fist-bumping lady friend looks forward to my weekly arrival. She seems thrilled to dispense unusual non-edible materials that for some reason are donated, or have expired in some unique way. Bars of soap made out of sugar. Bamboo toothbrushes—the lightest handles with the softest bristles. A glass mug engraved with the words: ENJOY THE MAGIC OF CHRISTMAS! One day she handed me a three-by-five card on which she had personally written these words: *"I can tell you are a worrier. Throw all your anxiety onto Him, because He cares about you. Cast your burden on the LORD—He will support you! Don't be anxious about anything; rather, bring up all your requests to God in your prayers and petitions along with giving thanks. Then the peace of GOD that exceeds all understanding will keep your heart and mind safe in Christ Jesus."*

Of course, I thanked her. Clearly the people at this church want me to enjoy life. They give me gifts, they welcome me, they wear masks to protect me from the pandemic, they invite me back, they bless me and bless me. Who else does this? Who else wants me to have happiness? I'm a Jewish girl, but I've never known the rewards of religion. Is it too late?

❁

My age presents challenges, though the internet tells me I have a good chance of living to ninety. But the road ahead for me is filled with so many medical tests. My doctor, who during the covid pandemic doesn't actually see her patients but communicates only by video-call or email, ordered a series of blood tests for me. Since my breast cancer surgery ten years ago, she requires me to have a CEA test which tracks a cancer marker. She called to inform me that my recent test's results were concerning: my antigens were elevated. She duly ordered another and after I had my blood drawn at the lab, (both the tech and I wearing our masks), she called to inform me they had risen further. Duty bound, she then referred me to an oncologist, who, without ever seeing me clinically, ordered yet another test, a CT/Pet scan.

✿

Though the date was set for the new test, the day for a previously ordered test, my colonoscopy, was approaching. Before I could have the colonoscopy, I was required to take a COVID-19 test. To do this, I had to drive to the clinic whose drive-through line wrapped several times around the parking lot.

While slowly inching forward, I sneezed. As I leaned sideways to grab the handkerchief on the passenger seat, my foot briefly slipped off the brake pedal and I hit the car in front of me. Hit it very softly. The impact was very soft, but it was a bump. The woman ahead leapt out of her car and strode furiously toward me. She was baring her teeth. I turned off my ignition and got out of my car. I checked her bumper. Not a scratch. The line ahead was now moving forward, and the cars behind us began to honk.

"You crazy bitch, you fucking bitch!" She stood close to me, wearing a nurse's badge. "You hit me! I'll sue you!"

"I'm sorry," I said. "But there's no damage."

"The whole fucking world is damaged," she yelled.

She *hmphed* away, shaking her fist in the air. I returned to my car, started the engine. Moved forward. Stopped. Another nurse stuck a long Q-tip up each of my nostrils, and jabbed another one into the back of my throat.

COVID-negative, my reward was to drink the ten gallons of lemon-flavored liquid in preparation for my colonoscopy. In the pre-op room, I could hardly wait for the anesthetist's infusion of propofol. I remembered, with gratitude, the same moment before previous procedures—for my gall bladder surgery, for my hysterectomy surgery, for my breast cancer surgery, for my knee replacement surgery. Why not just get put out for good and be done with it all! With all the tests to come, and the waiting for results and the fear, followed by even more tests! We will all fail the ultimate test, so why keep going? Can't an old woman get some propofol for at-home for domestic use?

✿

For the CT/Pet scan, I would be injected with a radioactive material, and have to wait an hour for it to circulate through my body. My husband drove me to the special imaging complex that did MRIs, CTs, ultrasounds, digital mammography, nuclear medicine, fluoroscopy, and guided biopsies. As he drove, I took a picture of his profile. I always have my camera ready in case something amazing passes us by, but my husband is often the only subject available. I've acquired hundreds of these photos of him driving us to supermarkets and medical appointments, but also through the Tuscan hills outside Florence where he once taught for a term, and through the moors of England when we spent his sabbatical year in Oxford, and on Highway 101 through California where the ocean breeze ruffled our hair through the car's sunroof. His handsome profile had changed considerably since the last time I took pictures of him driving—his cheeks now were visibly sunken, his hair had thinned, his beard's stubble was completely white. His beautifully-shaped lips seemed narrowed into a tight line. What was happening to him? And though I meant to take only photos of the subject in front of my camera lens, I sometimes accidentally took a selfie and realized that whatever was happening to my husband was also happening to me.

❋

The CT tech, a middle- aged man who introduced himself as Jimmy, called me into his office. He asked me to leave all my belongings with my husband and told me to follow him down the hall. "I'd like to take my phone," I told him, "So I can read if I have to wait an hour."

"Take nothing with you. You are going to just have to relax while you wait."

Relax again? While waiting for radioactive material to light up places in my body where cancer might be growing? My husband threw me a pitying glance and took out his copy of the *New Yorker*.

Just as I was about to recline on a soft chair, Jimmy came in and whispered: "Don't worry about getting through this hour. In a few minutes I'll be back, and I'll tell you my life story."

I wondered how to pass the time. I tried to meditate, which lately I had been practicing with a Zoom class. The key to success- ful meditation was to choose an anchor, ideally your own breath going in and out, and hang onto the anchor no matter how wildly your thoughts might flit about. In meditation, we were encouraged to accept ourselves in whatever state we were in at the present mo- ment. To be at peace without criticizing ourselves was the way to enter a transformative process. I was just getting into the rhythm of it—my breath going out like a little death, and then coming in as a blessing, over and over again—when Jimmy came back into my room and said, "Now I have time between patients and I can tell you how I got this job, how I always wanted to be a jet pilot, how I came to this country from Lebanon and found the most beautiful woman in the world to marry." I pretended to listen, while still fo- cusing on my breath. Finally, I begged to know if the radioactive stuff was now sufficiently distributed through my body and could we please have the scan.

Jimmy ushered me into the room which he said had to be kept very cold since the multimillion-dollar scanner was temperamental and easily overheated. It looked like a cylindrical refrigerator laid on its side, into which I had to be strapped. Jimmy's narration of his life story had ended happily with a double wedding at which both he and his brother married the two most beautiful women who were, like the brothers, also from Lebanon. He told me to hold still, he was about to start the scan. He turned out the light in the room and closed the door. A motor turned on and I could feel something whizzing above my head. I lost the anchor of my breath at once, since meditating in a dark freezing tube was like meditating in a coffin. I hated being in this situation but I tried to accept myself and appreciate my hatred.

✣

Fury sits in a pouch somewhere and shoots out suddenly when you least expect it. It's a crack on the skull with a hatchet. It can strike while you're putting on your socks, or as you catch a glimpse of cable news.

Fury seems a reasonable reaction to the delivery of a big carton from Walmart with only a single jar of jelly in it but the wrong flavor. To a mistaken letter from the IRS informing me that I owe $4000. To a robo-call that insists I have been charged by Amazon for a new iPhone and I need to press 1 to cancel the charges. To news that my truck warranty has expired and I need to renew it. To the sound of my grandson calling but it isn't really him: "Hello Grandma, you may not recognize my voice since I have a cold, but I've been in a car accident and I need your help."

Old traumas also rise up suddenly, painful enough to bring tears to my eyes—my husband's mother who hated my guts because she thought I was too thin and not rich enough for her son. Who, with her husband, tried to throw me down the stairs when we told them we were engaged! Who, when I finally married her son, looked at my delicate, beautiful thin gold wedding band and said,

"Such a skinny ring! What's the matter, are you ashamed of being married?"

Fury at the bastard who reviewed my first novel, published when I was in my twenties that told the story of my father's tortured death by leukemia at the age of fifty-five. I got the exciting news from my publisher that TIME magazine was to a review my book. The magazine sent a photographer to my home to take pictures of me sitting at my typewriter, holding my baby daughter in my arms, and standing beside my handsome husband. For once, I felt lucky. A review in TIME could make my name! The photographer stayed all day. He asked me to change my clothes three times; he asked me to pose in the back yard sitting on the swing, holding a flower; he. asked if I could make him a tuna fish sandwich.

When, a week later, I read the review, I nearly fell to my knees:

> . . . *Abram Goldman is a robust and endearing antique dealer with an imaginative zest for life. When he begins to suffer from leukemia, he is treated with the inevitable escalation of drugs, yet his condition deteriorates. His Jewish-mother-type wife and daughters—one, the narrator, married with two daughters; the other, the novel's problem child, unmarried and with one foot in the Beat Scene—observe his gallant but losing battle.*
>
> *Such a tale is, of course, depressing. But Author Merrill Joan Gerber makes it even more so by coating it with sentimentality. A short-story writer who has published in* Redbook *and* Mademoiselle, *she seems glued to the traditional women's magazine faith—the world is blackest just before a rose-tinted dawn. After the Abram's death, the problem sister marries her beatnik lover. The other sister decides that she will bear a son with her father's name— "It was all I could do in this world-all I could hope to do." Almost any death has a quantum of emotion, but because this author writes from a self-pitying, self-absorbed point of view, she grabs most of it for herself!*

Fury! Jewish-mother-type wife? The man misunderstood every word in my book. A moron! A woman-hater! An asshole! And TIME magazine printed not one single picture!

❖

My old age brings on anger. Let's look at it full in the face, the face that now has become a wreckage of my former smooth cheeks, lovely lips, delicate neck, blue eyes, flawless earlobes, chestnut-colored hair. And below, my once-gracefully shaped body, with a dancer's arms and legs, adorable breasts, firm bottom—what's become of it now? An elephant in a nightgown! And inside? The uterus gone, a breast disfigured, a knee missing, a bladder that leaks, a heart that bursts into tachycardia without warning, and my god, the horrifying whiskers on my chin.

What is this punishment for? Punishment is for being bad, of course. My grandmother told me to be a good girl all the time because God would know when I was bad and would punish me. When I was five and in kindergarten, I was instructed by my teacher to go up the stairs to the principal's office at P.S. 238 in Brooklyn—the place where only bad children were sent. I went up those stairs shaking with terror I could feel in every cell of my body. When I entered the principal's office, he handed me a snapshot of myself in the schoolyard wearing a little hankie pinned to my coat as I stood with two other children playing a game and said, "Hello dear little girl, the school photographer took this photo, and here is a copy for you and your family."

❖

There's a picture of my husband and me taken in Miami Beach outside our high school's theater at an evening concert where my husband was an usher. As a volunteer, he got to attend concerts for free, and on this night, our first real date, he planned to let me in a side door so we could both watch a famous pianist perform. He was wearing the required white jacket and looked so astonishingly handsome that when I saw him, I felt an actual weakness in my knees. I was newly sixteen, I was thin, with curly brown hair, and I wore a gold four-leaf clover necklace (a gift from my father) in the square-cut neckline of my dress.

Studying that picture in later years, I think my husband looks a bit like Elvis Presley or Tony Curtis, but on that night, he was just my gorgeous new boyfriend. As I sat beside him in the dark row of the concert hall, he slowly slid his arm along the back of my chair and touched my shoulder with his fingers. I gasped.

After the concert, but a half hour before my father was to pick me up in front of the theater, my boyfriend and I walked down to the beach and sat in the moonlight by the ocean. He reached for something on my neckline, (I thought my four-leaf clover), and he said "Mine?"

Thinking he meant the necklace, I said, "No!" but what he was really saying was "Mind?"—did I mind him touching me there where my small breasts were blooming? My saying *no* gave him permission to touch them gently, first one, then the other. I knew then that he must touch them forever.

❈

My husband and I keep visiting retirement communities. My God, I don't want to live in two rooms, with my husband in the next room with his piano or in the room with me. I don't want to attend lectures, exercise classes, or learn origami. I don't want to eat every meal surrounded by other old folks. Although it's true I am so very tired of cooking all our meals, I can't see that paying ten thousand dollars a month to be rescued from that chore is worth the cost.

When my husband and I visit these various retirement communities, we briefly forget that at home we have a ten-room house filled from one end to the other with the essential objects from our fifty-odd years of living there. We sometimes talk about the practical benefits of moving into one of these expensive retirement units, packing only a few articles of clothing, a couple of books, even a bathing suit (all these places have pools), and moving into a totally neat room or two, with the promise of having whatever color of paint on our walls that we choose, and having them install any color carpet that we want.

The concept is deliberately, intentionally inviting—just us, a few necessary things, and excellent meals prepared for us every day. A new, inviting social world, maid service, entertainment, instruction, a personal gym, a beauty shop, as well as promises of emotional tranquility, safety and protection, transportation to medical care if necessary, and a subtext that it's likely we will be so much healthier in this supportive, welcoming community, that we'll never be sick.

Sometimes I imagine that our entire house has vaporized—not a thing left, as happens when a plane crashes into a home. Not a single photo album remaining, not an obsolete pile of computers, no tax records, medical bills, vinyl records, videotapes, cassette tapes, reel-to-reel movies, CDs or eight tracks. Gone would be our stacks of the *New Yorker,* the *New York Review of Books,* the *Sewanee Review,* the *Atlantic Monthly.*

Lost sock drawers would be dispatched, never to be sorted through again. Closets of extension cords, hammers and pliers, miscellaneous bulbs, plugs, rolls of tape—vanished! Let me out of here with just the clothes on my back. Immigrants have faced such a bleak landscape for centuries. Our grandparents did it, why not us? With our bare bones, why not venture into a new life?

But once we get home after such a visit, once we enter our cluttered, familiar, messy place, we begin to cherish our space, in which we can wander, fortunate as we are: my husband to his music room, where his grand piano sits and his pile of precious volumes of Bach's music; me to my sewing room (where I have not sewed in forty years), where my mother's sewing box sits with its red tomato pincushion, its container of unique buttons, its seamripper, and her silver thimble pocked with tiny dots. Even her black wooden darning egg with which she showed me how to darn holes in my father's socks is in there. A skill to remember, she told me.

Our house: container of all memories, events, emergencies, place of all meals, of our thousands of nights of falling asleep together in our bed, of telling our daughters their bedtime stories, of standing grateful, under the showerhead to be washed clean of the day's stains, real and imagined.

What? Move to a retirement place where the old who preceded you in that clean, repainted apartment are dead? Might have actually died in there?

The real terror is this. Which of us will die first? (It stands to reason he will.) Which of us will be able to survive in this house all alone? Who will open the jar of blueberry jam? (Me needing him.) Who, when the pipe bursts under the sink, will have the presence of mind to go outside to find that green wheel and turn off the water? (Him needing me.)

But I also know that we are old, isolated, losing interest in all things, even each other, and that we almost never see another human being in a social context. We are not joiners. We are Jews without a Jewish community. We don't believe in God, or heaven, or an afterlife, or even in having funerals. Who are these people who have two hundred guests at their funerals? They seem to be rich guys who traveled the world, flew their own planes, invented the zipper, gave their wives diamonds, and have brilliant, successful children. And who are we? No one.

Not really no one, because we, too, have lived long, interesting lives, we have had children (but where are they?) and we did a few important things, like work, and teach, and write a book, and be nice to some people, and help a few to achieve some goal or other, but still, who would come to a funeral of either of us? Why would we want anyone to come?

My husband's parents' ashes are in the back of a closet at his sister's house. She keeps intending to scatter them somewhere, sometime, and now that she could add her husband's ashes to the mix as well, she still never gets around to it. Her husband shot himself in the head in their back yard when he realized he was becoming helpless. He knew how to use a gun; he'd been in the Korean war. He told his wife what he was planning. She knew it. She knew what he was going to do the day he went out into the backyard in his bathrobe with his gun. He was suffering three fatal diseases at once and he was aware he was a few days short of total dependence on others. She waited for the sound of the gunshot. She waited. And she waited. Then she heard him calling her name. Oh, she knew he might not do it, and that would mean total servitude to him for the rest of her life. She was terrified he would do it, and also feared he might not. And when he called her name, she went to the garden door to ask him what he wanted. He said, "I can't find the bullets." She said, "Look in your bathrobe pocket." He looked and said, "Oh yes, thank you." And then she went inside, and she heard the gunshot. Even so, the police checked her hands for gunpowder just in case.

My husband and I don't want funerals though he once said he wished his parents had graves somewhere that he could visit if he wanted to. Since their graves are still in his sister's closet, he decided we should buy funeral plots even if we don't want funerals. In fact, we already own four graves for the two of us. We bought two expensive plots in the Jewish cemetery in Hollywood Hills when my mother died and was buried beside my father, and then we bought two more cheap plots in the little graveyard—the Pioneer Cemetery in our small town, established in 1881, a block down the road from our house. It spans two acres and features magnificent oak trees. We walk through that cemetery very often. We breathe the same air in our house that blows gently over the graves in that cemetery. The oak trees growing there are so tall that they nearly block our view of the mountains that rise just to the north. We appreciate our little cemetery because it has no gift and flower shop, no piped music, no rules about embalming or having a cement enclosure for each coffin. It has no worker collecting little printed cards signed by funeral guests as they exit a fancy chapel in time to see a coffin containing a body being slid into a shiny black hearse for the trip to the gravesite.

In fact, our cemetery overlooks a park where little kids ride on swings, and where families picnic and where dog-lovers play with their dogs. It hardly reeks of death at all. At Christmas we see poinsettias decorating the graves, and on the fourth of July, the city parade passes right by the buried dead, music blasting from big speakers as the owners of old Fords and Pontiacs wave to the people lining the street, the Search and Rescue team marches by with its sweet, slavering dogs and the fire trucks roar by, shooting darts of water at the onlookers on what is usually a very hot day. For a cemetery, it's really a cheerful place. Sometimes, when there's a burial, the sounds of a bagpipe come floating down the street toward our house. It's a sweet place, and seems it would be homelike for us to be buried there.

❈

Sometimes I wonder if, in our old age and loneliness, we decide to join a synagogue, and we get to have a rabbi. Will we have to then be buried in the Jewish cemetery alongside my parents? Will someone have to say the kaddish for the dead over our graves? Should we learn the words of the kaddish ourselves so that one of us can say kaddish for the other? I looked up the translation of the kaddish prayer itself. How could it be that it never mentions dying?

Glorified and sanctified be God's great name throughout the world which He has created according to His will.

May He establish His kingdom in your lifetime and during your days, and within the life of the entire House of Israel, speedily and soon; and say, Amen.

May His great name be blessed forever and to all eternity.

Blessed and praised, glorified and exalted, extolled and honored, adored and lauded be the name of the Holy One, blessed be He, beyond all the blessings and hymns, praises and consolations that are ever spoken in the world; and say, Amen . . .

The kaddish for the dead is asking quite a bit. Should we be required to bless and praise, glorify and exalt, extoll and honor the holy one, especially since the holy one has just allowed our beloved person to die?

❀

What if one of us falls? I've had one very serious fall. It happened on a day I was planning to go to my therapy group at the medical clinic. Our therapist had confessed to me a love of lemons. We had a lemon tree in our backyard. Our therapist was in her late fifties, about the age of my oldest daughter, unmarried, good-looking with dyed red hair that fell in a strange pointy cut on either side of her face. She counseled five depressed patients, including me, who met with her each week. Every one of us was dealing with some form of mental illness: PTSD, bi-polar disorder, an eating disorder, a panic disorder or suicidal thoughts. I personally had considered drowning myself in our pool for no clear reason that I could recall. My husband thought my depression might be due to my car accident, which occurred on a day I was on my way to the Cancer Support Center for my painting class. By that time, my chemo was over, my radiation completed, and a fairly large part of my left breast had been removed. During my recovery, I continued to drive to the support center for a healing art class.

The art teacher showed us wonderful ways to paint palm fronds, but I painted only images from my family photo album—my grandmother as a girl after arriving in America from Poland, wearing a black lace dress pulled tight at her waist. My mother in her eighth-grade graduation dress in a photographer's studio in Brooklyn, a diploma in her hands and on her breast a small gold pin inscribed with her name and the words ACADEMIC EX-CELLENCE AWARD." My father, my beloved, died-too-soon father, wheeling me in a carriage on the Coney Island boardwalk, he smoking his pipe, and I teething on another of his pipes' stems—an actual white wooden pipe of his in my tiny mouth. My mother and father at the Bronx Zoo with me, the three of us in front of a cage of wild animals, while in my gloved hand I hold a box of Cracker Jacks.

Driving to my painting class one day, my car was suddenly hit from behind by a truck and sent spinning around to face oncoming traffic! I felt myself sailing through the air, spun around to see trucks speeding toward me and then one of them smashed into my car, then another. I felt the windshield glass crumble into my lap.

I was transported from the car to an ambulance and then to a hospital. I was injured, but not badly. But the accident unmoored me. I had just survived cancer and then—when the truck smashed into me—I found myself having to face death again.

I began to think I had lived long enough. I wandered the edge of our pool, wondering how long it would take to drown. I counted all my pills saved over the years from my many surgeries . . . phenobarbitals, Vicodins, Valiums, tramadols, Norcos, Ativans. When my husband saw me reading my old copy of *Final Exit*, published by the Hemlock Society, he convinced me to see a psychiatrist. She encouraged me to join my therapy group which was the reason that on the day of my fall I was going into my backyard to pick a lemon from our tree to give to my therapist.

A lovely large lemon on the back side of the tree caught my attention. I pulled on the fruit but it would not release into my hand. I pulled even harder. The branch of the tree shook, but the lemon held on. I used all my strength. The lemon snapped free, sending me backwards so fast that I fell over a brick planter and landed on my back in the dirt, smashing my head against the wall of the house behind it.

My husband, hearing me yell, came out and at first could not find me, invisible as I was behind the tree and hidden in the weeds of the planter. He tried to pick me up but he could not; only his fingers remained strong from playing the piano.

I told him to call our nephew, a very tall young man. Though I had to lie there in the planter for another hour, my nephew arrived, all six-foot -four of him, and lifted me up in the blink of an eye. However, I did not get to my therapy group that day with a lemon for my therapist because I had broken a vertebra. Man proposes, God disposes.

✻

My friend at the food bank began to worry about my health when I told her I had to have a biopsy of my thyroid. The scan results had announced the following:

> *Conclusion: Hypodense right thyroid lobe suspicious for hyperme-tabolic neoplastic pathology and thyroid carcinoma. There is intense tracer activity in the region of the urinary bladder.*

When I emailed my oncologist, she sent me a happy-face emoji. All that tracer activity in the urinary bladder was simply the radioactive material being peed away. As for the thyroid—well, yes, tracer activity there might mean cancer. She advised another biopsy in three months. If it was cancer, we'd deal with it. Forget it for now.

Forget it?

❊

I wish my husband would remember to take out the garbage. To change a light bulb. To put a new water filter in the ice-maker. To pick up animal poop. One morning we found the garbage can knocked over and the remains of a week's worth of trash littering the front yard. Bears have been coming down from the mountains where there's been no rain and food is scarce. Neighbors' security cameras catch them climbing into their pools and up their avocado trees. On the day our trash was strewn everywhere, I noticed what looked like an enormous turd on our lawn. I studied this huge, seg-mented thing and wondered if I should take a photo of it with my cell phone, maybe examine it through the lens app to confirm it was actually produced by a bear. When I told my husband I wanted to take a photo of it, he looked at me with his eyebrows raised. I knew he disapproved of the idea. It seemed unseemly to him. I was always willing to cross lines he would not venture past.

A week later, the thing was still on the lawn. When my husband and I went out to take our walk, I pulled a long twig from a tree and knocked the pieces of shit, over and over, till I got them all the way to the curb, where on Monday the street cleaning truck would swoop them up with a big brush and take them away. But when I saw my husband watching me knocking the poop around with my stick, when I saw the puzzlement and dismay on his face, I won-dered if our marriage was finally coming to an end.

❉

My husband has allowed me to cut his hair every month for the last fifty years. This shows some trust. I learned how to cut hair when I was five, in my aunt's little beauty shop which was in a bedroom in our Brooklyn house, where she served the neighborhood ladies. My aunt dedicated herself to the wartime efforts in Brooklyn; she sold war bonds, she rolled bandages for the soldiers, she marched with the Red Cross women in parades on Avenue P, all of them dressed in white, like angels. From her customers, she collected little trinkets—beads, pearls, costume jewelry—which would be distributed to fliers whose planes might crash on a mountain top in New Guinea and it would become necessary to trade with natives for food. My aunt and her customers talked incessantly about the war, their husbands or sons who were off fighting, the food rationing, the latest news from various fronts, all the while my aunt's scissors would be clipping, cutting, and dancing around the heads of these worried women. As a child, I listened to their stories, I bent fallen hairpins into the shapes of animals and learned enough to cut my own hair and the hair of my future husband ever after.

Now, once a month, I roll a kitchen chair into our little bathroom, and my husband removes most of his clothes and sits before me while I cut his hair with a pair of antique scissors rescued from my aunt's beauty shop. I proceed from the tender back of his neck to the edges of his ears, to the top of his head (now with barely a hair upon it), and finally to the front of his face where I trim his eyebrows, carefully, with a much smaller pair of scissors. With a little electric clipper, I shape his sideburns. Sometimes, when I am this close to him, he leans forward and kisses me wherever his lips land. Sometimes he lifts my shirt and he kisses my breast. I kiss the top of his head and hold it against me. We are so lucky to be together, alive, and at this old age, still taking care of one another. I want us to live together forever. Or even better, maybe die at the same time.

❄

I am struck with an idea for a new business; I will finally become an entrepreneur. I will call my company The End of the Road, and it will be a service for newly bereaved widows or widowers who wanted to skip the horrors of being the one left behind with all the crap to take care of, with all the financial details to sort out, the one who has to call the mortuary, order the coffin, throw out her husband's old shoes and give away his shirts and hats, the one who has to call tax lawyers, realtors, trust fund managers. My new business will simply be a kind of gentle transition—not the kind that transitions the grieving mate to a retirement community and arranges for the furniture to be laid out in her new one- room life but will provide a much-needed service for painless self-deliverance, the kind of end a sick well-cared-for dog enjoys. My company will provide fast and guaranteed death while at the same time contracting to take charge of all the requirements of ordering the death certificates, remodeling the run-down house and selling it for a big profit, assuring that the house and all its contents will be sold to the highest bidder and that one's heirs will get their rightful shares.

My new business will allow those who sign up to skip all the end-of-life horrors. Even better, my "premium" level of service could be chosen by both mates at the same time. On a selected date, together they'd check into a spa-like cozy place, together, with Baroque music playing, they'd clasp hands as a stream of propofol would be sweetly, painlessly administered to each, followed by a boost of fentanyl—and poof, all things unpleasant would vanish, especially the horror of protracted dying. Nothing left, nothing to it, nothing but sweet nothings now and forever.

✻

My kind friend at the food bank had new gifts to press upon me. A bag of modern, brightly colored, silicon soup ladles, with price labels attached, $15.95. Each! "What am I supposed to do with so many?" I asked her. "Be a good neighbor," she suggested. She handed through my window a super-size container of laundry detergent. "Listen to this," she said, and read to me from the label: "The uplifting scent of orange essential oil blended with essence of grapefruit and note of lemon and exotic citrus bursting with sunshine will brighten your mood. Smile and take on the day with your refreshingly clean laundry. So concentrated that only an eighth of a cup will do a large load of clothes!"

"It almost makes me want to do the laundry," I laughed. As I was about to drive away, she said, "Wait! One more gift!" and put into my hand me a small, leather-bound book titled *And He Walks with Me: 365 Daily Reminders of Jesus's Love.*

"I want you to keep this. I've underlined the most important parts on every page. Read a page every day. If you're sad, my friend, or scared, just remember, those who know Jesus as their friend are never alone. You will always have a friend in Jesus. And a friend in me."

"But what if you need it?" I asked her. "Don't worry. I have the whole bible!" she assured me, and we fist-bumped one more time.

✻

I keep my laundry in my pink and yellow seersucker college laundry bag on a hook in my sewing room; my husband keeps his in his Air Force duffel bag that hangs on a hook in his closet.

When I was aware that we probably both had no clean clothes left to wear, I normally would ask him to bring his laundry bag into the laundry room (where I assumed he would put his clothes into the washer). Though he seemed to hear me ask this, he also seemed to forget my request immediately. In the most recent enactment, I began asking him on Sunday to bring in his laundry. I usually make my request while we are eating a meal together, the time when we're most likely to exchange information. I asked him again on Tuesday if he would bring in the laundry so I could do a wash. He agreed. He didn't do it. I wondered if I would need to lead him by the hand to the hook in his closet. What was it about this simple request that made it so hard for him to process? Of course, I could easily have done it myself, delivered both his laundry and mine into the washing machine, but I didn't. I thought he should bring in his own dirty laundry. By Friday, I asked him, with some impatience, if he would now, this minute, bring in the laundry, that I was totally out of clean clothes and had to do a wash. "I've asked you several times," I reminded him, "so do it right now, will you?" "I will," he nodded, and then I watched him walk down the hall to practice the piano.

There are limits, even in a marriage of over sixty-two years, that can be breached. How many times do Bach's French Suites need to be played, no matter how beautifully and artistically and precisely when a family's underwear needs to be washed, dried, and folded? How much patience toward a partner, how much kindness and understanding of his needs, tolerance of his basic nature, acceptance of his human faults, even in view of one's adoration of his solid psyche, marvelous strong chin line, masculine handsomeness, prior sexual prowess—how much can a wife tolerate, finally? Not enough, apparently. Which brought me, at last, to throw at him the question growing ever more insistently in my bosom since I first met him one day before my sixteenth birthday. The question, shaped like a snake, came shooting out of my mouth when he came into the kitchen to take his heart and blood-pressure pills. "I have to know something. I've thought about this from the day I met you. Did you ever have sex with another woman? Did you do sexual things with some girl before me?"

He blanched. I never knew what that was until I saw it happen.

Holding onto his pill bottle, he said, "Why are you asking me this now?"

"Because, if I should have cancer again, I want to know the answer before I die. When you married me, I was pure as the fallen snow. I never, never, never—"

"Of course," he said. "I know that." He made a move toward me, as though he might pat me reassuringly, even tenderly, on my shoulder, but I jumped back.

"I wasn't even sixteen but you . . . you were eighteen! Older. More experienced. Please tell me! *Did* you have sex with some girl before me?"

I watched his eyes, the tilt of his head, as he thought about what to reply to me. He appeared to think I had gone crazy. I understood his hesitancy: many men of eighty-five—even of fifty-five or thirty-five—have had multiple, maybe dozens, maybe hundreds of women, girlfriends, lovers, wives, and here I wanted a total confession, one that might un-man him and his right to his own secrets, his own private knowledge of his manly history. He had a right to his secrets, didn't he? At that moment I didn't think so. From this man, to whom I had given myself in utter innocence, I wanted a pledge of his total loyalty and purity as well. We never would have gotten to this moment if only he had brought in the fucking laundry.

The look of anguish on his face revealed his unspoken reaction: that's enough. I can't do this. I can't listen any longer. As he turned to walk away, I knew I'd lost this final opportunity.

"From now on do your own laundry!" I cried out, helplessly, in tears. "I won't ever ask you again." I heard for one instant the pure madness in my voice.

"Oh, please, please," he pled, even as he turned to walk away from me, as he shuffled down the hall, as he struggled to get to his music room. "Please can't you just relax," he begged, talking to me over his shoulder while escaping from me. "You have been the love of my life. You have been my sweetheart forever." His head was shaking with the tremor from which he suffered so badly. "Please don't do this to us now," he said, "when there is so little time left for us to be happy."

True Believer:
My Friendship With Cynthia Ozick

IN JUNE, 1965, Cynthia Ozick reviewed my first book of short stories, *Stop Here, My Friend*, in *Midstream* magazine. "This," Cynthia wrote, "is a book about contemporary American Jews; so, of course, it is not a very 'Jewish' book . . . There are unmistakable Jewish signs and scenes here . . . there is a steerage courtship that revolves around a herring . . . a rich uncle dies in Brooklyn and a *kaddish* is said, an overindulgent mother flies up from Florida, unwanted, to help her daughter with her firstborn. In spite of all this, Miss Gerber's stories are without what is usually referred to as 'Jewish consciousness.' . . . Miss Gerber is a member of an expanding host, all these young Jewish writers who are turning out Jewish-flavored stories with nothing Jewish in them but the odor of the corner delicatessen . . . Perhaps, for once, they, like Miss Gerber, should bypass *Redbook* and strike out for the Red Sea."

When I read the review I felt not only a blow, but an insult as well—a dismissal by a woman writer of a woman who published stories in women's' magazines. In the sixties, these publications were shining beacons inviting fiction from women writers. *Redbook*, *Good Housekeeping*, *Ladies' Home Journal*, *McCall's*—all invited us to send our work directly, no agents needed. *Redbook* alone published four stories a month as well as a novella. Sylvia Plath wrote to her mother that she yearned to be published in the *Ladies' Home Journal*.

After *Stop Here, My Friend*, I published other books and stories in the following years, many having to do with my childhood memories of growing up in Brooklyn, with tales of my grandmother's journey from Poland to America, in steerage, at the age of seventeen, to escape the terrors unfolding in her shtetel at home. When I was a little girl, she taught me simple words of Yiddish while my aunt supervised my cooking of kreplach and mandelbrot. Each fall, my father came home from the Avenue N shul on Yom Kippur, fasting, unshaven, yet exalted in some way. My flyer cousin, "The Lost Airman," was shot down by Japanese Zeros over New Guinea and his younger brother, fighting Hitler in the European theater, had his leg destroyed by shrapnel as he flew a bomber over Germany.

When reviews of my books were published, I read them tentatively, fearing I might once again come upon a comment like the words of Cynthia Ozick: "Nothing Jewish in them." In every house on my Brooklyn Street lived Jews—and in many windows were gold stars.

Eighteen years after Cynthia spoke her judgement about my failings in *Midstream*, a friend called to tell me Cynthia Ozick would be speaking at one of the Claremont Colleges, that she and her husband were going and that I should go with them. "Not for me," I said.

"Oh, just come with us, it should be interesting."

I don't recall exactly what Cynthia spoke about that night, but her talk had the same accusatory tone she'd used in the review of my book, asserting that there were Jews with a genuine Jewish consciousness (Orthodox Jews, like herself), and that there were the "other" Jews. In the question-and-answer period, a man of serious demeanor raised his hand. "I am a Reform Rabbi," he said. "If Jews were under attack, would you accept me into your fortress?" Cynthia replied without hesitation that in all honesty she could not. The rabbi stood and walked out.

Following Ozick's talk, I walked with my friend to the table where Cynthia was signing books. Afterward, I found myself standing next to her as she was gathering up her papers and purse and

I said, "I'm a teacher and I have taught your story, 'The Shawl,' in my class."

"What's your name?" she asked.

I told her.

"Oh," she said, "I know who you are! I reviewed your book of stories. It was the first book review I ever did."

"Yes, and it was a stinging review."

"Oh no! I remember that I liked it."

"If you give me your address, I'll find a copy of the review and send it to you," I said. Cynthia willingly wrote her address for me and I gave her mine. Her voice was sweet and conciliatory, so different from the tone in which she had addressed the reform rabbi and others who had questioned her during her talk. "I'm sure you're wrong," she said, as we left the auditorium. "I'm sure I liked your book."

I wrote first:

February 15, 1983

Dear Cynthia—

Your review of Stop Here, My Friend *was in the June, 1965 Midstream. When I looked it up, I realized that there was really nothing I could do to correct my colorless, unhistoric Jewish way of life and furthermore, I was unwilling to leave* Redbook *for the Red Sea, since* Redbook *was helping to pay the bills . . . In fact, I am the daughter of a mother who held the old customs in contempt, who ridiculed them, and fooled my father once by substituting a pork chop for a lamb chop and then laughing because he didn't know the difference. She desired to become a genteel American woman like her gentile elementary school teachers. On the other hand, we lived with my aunt and grandmother who were reverent Jews, and committed to the importance of Jewish values (if sometimes confused about whether or not to eat Chinese food).*

Several times, after we moved to California with our children, we visited synagogues, intending to join one of them, but found we didn't have the impetus to stay on. When our daughters complained that the Sunday school teachers were often wrong about the Old Testament stories (since my husband is a history professor, they knew many of the basics already)—we just gave up.

From your talk last night, I realize you believe there are no excuses— I understand your conviction that the true and serious mode of a Jew is the Orthodox . . . but like any devotion, it has to be done with the whole mind and heart. In any case, despite my failings in your eyes, I was very glad to meet you.

Next time you come to California, I'd be happy if you called me.

Merrill Joan Gerber

❖

February 18, 1983

Dear Merrill Gerber,

I didn't remember anything negative in that long-ago review! . . . I have no copy of it, and wonder what it said. If it said something hurtful, that feels strange; because all these years I have kept your name as a writer of great gifts. I was tremendously glad to see how you have gone on, so prolifically, so richly; and I'll look up the novels I missed. Your mother substituting pork chops for lamb chops to "fool" your father was like Jacob, substituting himself for Esau, "The Hairy One," and out of Jacob came Israel! So your children or your children's children may yet form a redemptive generation . . . A Jew who eats a pork chop condones slavery and not just in Egypt . . .

I don't, by the way, speak out of "orthodoxy"—only out of continuity . . . Please read my Enlightenment essay in the February Commentary! *. . . It is true that "life as we live it is just another form of Jewish history"—but why the vessel without the content, why an empty pot?*

Cynthia Ozick

❋

March 3, 1983

Dear Cynthia—

I thought you might like to see the Midstream *review, so have made you a copy. Your review is not so different in theme from parts of your* Commentary *essay; the narrowness of the enlightened Jewish life. I don't see my enlightened life as narrow. When I hear Yiddish, my heart leaps. I lived in our home with my grandmother for fourteen years and she spoke very little English. Yet you might think I fell into enemy hands. When I went off to college at the University of Florida, I began to love literature and admire the minds of my non-Jewish professors who seemed to have a wider view of the world than my relatives in Brooklyn. My husband, who plays harpsichord, used to put on the phonograph a record of Bach's St. Matthew Passion and play it for hours a day when we were both going to grad school at Brandeis—and I felt we were traitors in some way. On the cover of the album was Christ himself, in agony. When my father came to visit and saw the album jacket, I was embarrassed. I think you were blessed with early focus: I suspect you never doubted your commitment. Certainly, by now, you are able to argue with the most learned of rabbis and scholars.*

Best, Merrill

Cynthia wrote back, and I replied at once. Within a month, we were engaged in a passionate correspondence about what it meant to be Jewish and whether we two, on opposite sides of the divide, could be friends. It took thirty-three more years to discover the answer.

On April 3, 1983, she wrote to me:

You write "with the friends I have that are not Jewish, I can only be myself perhaps . . . 50% of the time. Maybe less." What does this mean? What is being hidden? What is feared? Aren't we supposed to say the same thing to everyone? Otherwise, you end like St. Paul, the Great Hyp-

ocrite, who commends, and recommends, being all things to all people . . . It seems to me you've chosen the "liberalism" that brings culture to a dead end, and is left with nothing but the rags and tatters of memories of the immigrant generation's memories and experiences. Here we've just come through Passover: we've got a separate Passover kitchen in the basement. A consummation and a consuming: but after all it's about being FREE. There wasn't a single word in your letter that sounded like the utterance of a free human being. In fact, your description of what I take to be Jewish loyalties comes out as a denial of Passover, as a description of slavery . . . I don't ask forgiveness for my polemical passions; though I shouldn't care. You are free to relinquish it all. I shouldn't grieve for your children, though I desperately do. Please understand that I do understand that they are gifted and brilliant and sensitive and distinguished— how I don't want to lose them, because of their splendor!

All warm best, Cynthia

❊

April 17, 1983

Cynthia, I spent all day yesterday writing letters to you in my head. Whatever I write will be a muddle; you know your powers of argument are so formidable, and you are so obviously right, at least from your point of view, that there IS no argument.

But then I want to say, but. But I am not you, I did not have your experiences, I was not trained as you were trained, my path was not your path . . . You remember that Tevye sends away his daughter without saying goodbye; only his wife can show love. I have no patience with him, for whatever reasons he has! Reasons are not people.

I am angry that you would give me up, or that you say I write "like a stranger." I love many of the things you love; I share some of your past, if not all. I am more with you certainly than against you. But when everyone, God forbid, lines up in their personal fortresses, if you are at the gate of the Jewish city walls, you will turn me away because I don't want ANY fortresses, or walls, or hateful separations.

People turn away from you because they cannot face your wrath and your determination. They want your kindness and they get your disapproval and the fire in your eye. (I heard people talking as they left your lecture. Many have to turn away from such a force as yours.)

But I also find in you a sweetness, a great human love, and sensitivity to suffering which is exquisite. I don't know Biblical history as you do and I never will. I haven't time to make your subject my subject. I am still discovering my subject. I struggle every day. I can't let you take away from me what I feel is at my core after all, my Jewish identity (weak or meaningless though it may seem to you). If my children have great intelligence, it is their Jewish intelligence, and if they make beautiful things out of it for the world, it's real and it's fine and they're aware of where it comes from.

If I can't be honest in the Christian world, personally, I try to be honest in my writing, and in my letters to you. I don't feel I have no freedom, not while I can write . . .

I have a neighbor, a woman who used to wave to Hitler in parades. She is a good German hausfrau *and she has coffee in my house. I would help her if she called on me. I don't want to keep the fires of hate burning and I don't want to have to take my place in the fortress, holding a gun. Just as Jews were shot by Hitler for no other reason than they were Jews, Jews should be allowed no matter what to come into your circle because they are Jews.*

I invite you here any time. Love, Merrill

❁

April 22, 1983

Well, I can see that you & I can talk for a lifetime. So let's do that. Love, Cynthia

I think we were both delighted to find a companion who was eager to write long letters, several a week—whose ideas did not have to wait months or years for publication, but which could get an immediate response from the other within days. I was a fervent typist who could transform a thought to words with ease. Cynthia scrawled her letters to me mostly in script or sent postcards filled to the very edges as if bursting with words beyond their limits. I sent my letters in long green envelopes and watched with great anticipation for delivery of her little white envelopes addressed in her tiny writing.

April 28, 1983

Dear Cynthia—It's true we can't keep up this volley; I can sense we're both getting tired, and my feelings tell me I want to step over the net and work on your side . . . so why don't we proceed, tentatively (if you want to) as just little girls getting to know each other (God knows I always feel like a little girl, maybe you do, too) and maybe get to be friends. To start, I will send you pictures of all of us. My fifteen-year-old daughter (sixteen on Sunday) reads and re-reads Anne Frank's diary and cries, and has told me that she feels because Anne died so young, it's her duty, in a way, to live the kind of life Anne might have lived. (Do you think this is sentimental?) We could easily go on and on. I'd like to, at a slower pace, perhaps, less monumentally. It's scary here at the typewriter, and comforting to know you're there at your desk, chipping away at the dark.

 Love, Merrill

❉

May 3, 1983

Oh, those flowering, flowery daughters! The sixteen-year-old touches me. Merrill, not only do I always feel like "a little girl," I feel like an infant! Some mornings I re-enter the womb, where I certainly did like it. Will the grave be like that, contemplative, no responsibility? No, the womb is full of hope and solace, the grave empty. Putting a story away instead of sending it to The New Yorker?! Oh no. Publication hasn't anything to do with ego! It's simply finishing what you've written—it's the communication. It's unfair to wring a story from your heart and then hide it—it's unfair to the story. And its insights can't hurt; they can only illumine. All illumination turns, as you are helping me discover, into an embrace. . .You are so kind hearted, Merrill, that I see you must be the ideal mother. I have often been the wicked stepmother.

OK, let's not fight. OK, we're friends. Love, Cynthia

Cynthia and I endlessly discussed the pangs of writing, the indifference and cruelty of editors and agents, the growing up of our girls—my three daughters, and her one daughter, Rachel, who was the same age as my middle child. We discussed our domestic crises—squirrels in her attic, raccoons in mine, the problems of our bodies, my palpitations and her irritable bowel. She often mentioned that I was too engaged with the "quotidian"—the petty stuff of daily life—while she had bigger fish to fry. I knew she must have correspondents with whom she discussed political and metaphysical subjects, while I was engaged with raising three children, caring for a sick mother and aunt, cooking meals for my family and at the same time writing my stories and novels. For a time, she let the issues of Jewish loyalties lay quiet. We discussed our devotion to writing and our struggles. Her strident and argumentative tone mellowed—she was all about our being dear friends. By this time, Cynthia was writing me letters of recommendation for literary awards and commiserating with me over the rejections I received for a novel I'd written.

In 1982 my eldest daughter, Becky, married a man who was a member of the Unitarian Church. The wedding was in his church. No rabbi was present. Cynthia expressed horror when I told her he broke the traditional glass at the end of the ceremony. A few years later, she was again aghast when my youngest daughter, Susanna, won a Fulbright Scholarship to study in Germany. Upon hearing the news, Cynthia's immediate response to me was, "How can you let your child go to that cloaca of the world?" In 1990, when we were updating our old kitchen in the house, she wrote: "Speaking of which, I was dismayed to the depths that you are getting kitchen equipment from West Germany. They export poison gas equipment as easily as they do countertops, and with the same easy motives: money, money, money. Now comes the subject I shouldn't take up, Merrill. I love you too much to enter this old stuff again—it's just blown away, it isn't here, there's nothing but love and closeness and pleasure and admiration. Which you know. Yet I felt a stab when you said on the telephone something like, "You would feel terrible if Rachel had a Gentile boyfriend." The statement is true, but what stabbed me was your saying "You." I instantly thought of the child in the Haggadah who says "You," separating himself from the family. Your sister's tragedy came about partly because she fell into a mistake . . . but it also has something to do with turning away from the values of Study, Continuity, Menschlichkeit. Call it Heritage, or call it anything else, you know exactly what I mean. It's Joe, in short. And Becky's sorrows come from having married someone without the values of Study, Continuity, Menschlichkeit, Heritage. In a sense, she's fallen out of her "class."

It became impossible for me to debate these issues with Cynthia—my sister's and daughter's lives ruined because they chose not to marry Jews? Maybe I had some uncomfortable thoughts along those lines myself. Maybe.

In New York, at the Hadassah Harold U. Ribalow Award Ceremony for "The Kingdom of Brooklyn," on November 22, 1993, Cynthia Ozick spoke in my behalf. Here are excerpts from her comments:

> *Although this occasion is a literary celebration, and I will certainly be speaking of Merrill Joan Gerber's splendid body of work, I hope you will allow me to begin with a comment on friendship. This morning marks my third meeting with Merrill; we have looked into each*

other's eyes only twice before. Our telephone conversations have been so infrequent that even our voices carry the surprise of unfamiliarity . . . Is this really you? And yet we are entangled in the kind of intimacy, mutual spilling of beans, and sympathetic anxieties that usually arise out of proximity—the friendship that ripens over cups of tea. I think Merrill and I will be drinking tea today but not then again perhaps for years. So how did this come about? On what does it depend? The answer is that ours is an epistolary friendship, a patient one, one that grows at the glacial pace of the United States Post Office. Although Merrill owns, I believe, every newfangled machine ever invented—she has a photocopier, she has a fax, she even has a bread-making machine—our correspondence crawls through the mail, and when a letter finally arrives it is already marinated in history. Merrill has given me her history and her heart and I have given her mine.

But it wasn't always so. Our earliest acquaintance was hostile. Long, long ago, when Merrill's work first came to my attention—it was a collection of short stories called Stop Here, My Friend—*I wrote what must have been a mainly negative review. Today I remember almost nothing of what I said in that review. I probably complained that the characters although Jews were deficient in their Jewishness. That was my single direct encounter with Merrill for many years. When we finally met in person for the first time, in California, decades later, we instantly fell into a quarrel, which I'm afraid I started, on the whole question of Jewish viewpoint. It was I confess less a quarrel than a scolding—a one-sided assault on my part, aggressively intolerant. And even that wasn't enough—it all boiled over into letters. Back-and-forth the letters went, mine nasty and Merrill's nice, mine furiously polemical and Merrill's sweetly sane.*

Until one day I looked down at one of Merrill's replies and understood in a sudden blaze of common sense and of marveling that my correspondent was, of all the writers I've known, among the kindest, most insightful, and intuitive, the most psychologically sensitive, the most reasoning and responsible. And surely the most forgiving.

To these qualities I added another one that counts in literature as stringently as it counts in life. Merrill is, above all and underneath all, a crucially honest writer. She is honest in her letters. She is honest in her op-ed pieces and she is honest in her fiction. In a time overcome by fictive inconclusiveness and confusion Merrill Joan Gerber writes in pursuit of illumination and penetration.

But what about the Jews? Consider this generously abundant writer's last four books, which reveal the lives of contemporary Jews as they sometimes really are. Would I today want to argue with Merrill over whether her Jewish characters have conscious Jewish commitments or promise what we like to call Jewish continuity? Never. I revise and chastise and regret my old acrid self . . . The lives of Jews as they are lived before our bewildered and wondering eyes are as real as a table, a glass, an apple. The way we live now is the Jewish truth, and in the hands of a consummately honest writer will be drawn, as honesty always is, toward metaphysical grounds.

Of course, it was gratifying to hear that Cynthia had forgiven me what she considered my lapses and decided that my work provided, in its way, access to what she called "a Jewish truth." I considered once again the words Cynthia spoke: "I revise and chastise and regret my old acrid self." Could she have meant it? She had said it to a room full of Hadassah members and many Jewish friends and writers. Two of my daughters were there, one with her fiancé. Yet, I feared that at any moment she could and would strike out against me if I did not live up to her standards. I had the sense that she dismissed as worthless other Jewish writers who did not fit her definition of "real" Jews. Many of her own stories about Jewish lives were vibrant, humorous, delightful. Two of her tales, "The Shawl" and "Rosa," revealed her horror at the agonies of the holocaust. What she had learned about Hitler's concentration camps had shaped her view of life. Ten years older than I was, Cynthia experienced World War Two as a teenager. The nightmares, the killings, were real to her. She was just a year older than Anne Frank. Nothing was more important to her than Jewish commitments and ultimately the creation and survival of Israel. Yet, I lived with other visions, other attitudes, less exclusive, less stringent, less limiting than hers were.

The years passed along—I saved all of Cynthia's letters in white boxes with carbon copies of my letters paper-clipped to hers. When e-mail came into her life, in 2004, Cynthia took to the ease of it with delight, though she always claimed she was helpless with gadgets.

We both suffered periods of deep gloom.

June 19, 2004

Merrill—As for your having the blues: I did somehow sense it. And what we have to do with the dyings all around us, and the declines, is defy them and yell Never Mind! The job of the living is to live. The job of writers is to write, and what a lucky thing this is, when you look around and see how the great mass of humankind doesn't have this impulse, which lasts as long as life lasts: or anyhow until disability and death.

In time my children grew up. I buried both my mother and my aunt. In 1994, my middle daughter, Joanna, got married. While she was in college, she had met Cynthia's daughter, Rachel, when both were studying in Israel. Joanna's wedding, complete with rabbi, chupa, Klezmer band and dancing, delighted Cynthia. (Was this when she sent me a present—a sundial to put in the yard, with these words carved into it: "Count Only Happy Hours"?) Cynthia and I continued to live, as the saying goes, "in each other's mouths."

Then around the time of the coming election of 2008, something changed in the tone of Cynthia's letters:

June 9, 2008

Very dear Merrill,

"You are in my mind," you say beautifully and touchingly. And you are in my mind indelibly. But well, the thing you won't let into your mind are my political harangues! (When Obama won, I felt literally emotionally sick. His speech to Aipac had as its undercurrent: Unlike Bush, I'm preparing to twist your arm, Israel. And of course the backtrack on Jerusalem. What counts more, 'health care' (as if it doesn't exist in this country, or annihilation? Another harangue on the way, unless I can't manage to get it to you) . . . the last Democrat I voted for was Gore, but then he hadn't yet turned himself into Chicken Little.

    OK, so do you want to declare a moratorium on all political talk? Love! C

And then again from Cynthia, on June 26, 2008:

Happy Anniversary! The only other teenage romance I know of which culminated in very early marriage (at 19) didn't last. So what's the secret? My guess is Joe. You are the volatile one. Joe is the steady one. (Obnoxious kosher note—regarding your going to The Red Lobster for your anniversary dinner, even though you say you did not eat a lobster . . . No one would enter a Red Lobster restaurant if the creature were called what it actually is: Red Cockroach. Which is exactly what a lobster is: same species, myriapoda, only bigger. And both eat carrion.) (Another lovely subject.)

Now Cynthia began sending me page upon page of right-wing commentary, echoing in so many ways Fox News rants, which I essentially ignored, as I could see nothing to say in response. Obama's election had clearly affected her in a way I found hard to understand. The new President, she wrote, was a "Haman in the White House." Democrats, including Hillary Clinton, were bent upon Israel's demise, and thus Cynthia threatened me that I must not vote for a Democrat at any cost. Such polemics were not for me, and I was disappointed, to say the least, that we had veered so far from our original conversations about writing, art, family life, literature and friendship.

Then another letter arrived.

August 19, 2010

Very dear Merrill,

Finally, finally, you've uttered a solid fact. Two of them, in fact. One, you elected Obama and two, you couldn't stomach Palin. Instead of a pro-Israel stupid Palin, who would do the country and the Jews no harm (and couldn't have succeeded to the presidency, anyhow, given that McCain, no great brain either, is alive and well), you and Joe are now responsible for a clever, sly, shrew's ideologically radical Third-World-minded enemy of Israel. (Whereby you failed to avoid an equally stupid stumbling fool of a Biden as vice president.) Was the so-called health bill more precious than a president who was certain NOT to sell Israel down the river, a thing that was manifest in Obama from the very beginning? What, after all, is the first priority? Our grandchildren's lives. If the deep wounds Obama perpetrates aren't quickly stanched, their generation will be adrift in a country that is inimical to their well-being, and it has already begun. What do you think will be the position, or the condition, of American Jews should Israel go down?

Love, C

And worse was to come.

February 27, 2015

There is the anti-semite in the White House, and what are the consequences for the very near future if Jews naively, gullibly, and yes, robotically, vote for the Democrats in 2016? American Jews have already elected a Haman, so anything is possible. The German Jews at least had enough perspective not to vote for der Fuhrer (though many believed naively, gullibly and yes, robotically, that it would all pass); but Ameri-can Jews, content in our fleshpots, are likely to be fully self-destructive.

Purim is here. Mordechai says to Esther, Don't think that you, in the palace, are exempt! Hence, don't think that the foundation of hos-tility Obama is preparing within the Democratic Party will not hurt our grandchildren. To have America turn against Jews is deeply frighten-ing, and what Obama is doing is not, as you shockingly put it, Merrill, "wrong." It's dangerous.

Obama an anti-semite! Dangerous? Haman in the White House? Obama who spoke with sane, fluid intelligence, Obama with his fair-minded, compassionate belief that all people were worthy of respect and should be treated with kindness? I some-how had missed that he was a villain—I could find no evidence of it. How he loved his children (and other children), loved his wife and showed what a loving family life was about. How balanced he was, cool, thoughtful, brilliant. What had poisoned Cynthia's mind to have her spit like a snake when saying Obama's name? Her husband had fallen ill, she was chained to her home, she was embittered to a degree I couldn't fathom. On one hand, she was a supremely gifted writer. On the other, she was willing to de-mean me and to speak with undisguised contempt about persons who mattered deeply to me and to other decent persons. Why was I able to continue to remain her friend when she was showing, more and more, something like hatred for me, accusing me of betraying the Jews? Cynthia, a worldly and sophisticated person, now suddenly seemed to hover menacingly above me like my fa-ther's old-world mother, my angry grandmother Fanny, who had hated the name my mother gave me (not Jewish-sounding)—and, grabbing the baby, me, from my mother's arms, demanded that my mother change my name to Masha after some dead relative of hers. So that my mother had to snatch me back and, in the future, could not bear to bring me to see my father's mother.

Cynthia's home life, with a caretaker in the house for her husband, seemed to imprison and punish her.

May 14, 2015

A wasp in the kitchen, a big crazily flying thing. I struggled to swat it; nothing could stop the evil thing. Later, Miss Thompson, who stays the night, accidentally encountered it on the floor in the dark, and, wearing only socks, inadvertently stepped on it, and got stung! I have no pictures in the computer, and I have no laptop. I never look back to anything, unless it's for a specific need. Ah, 2008: the beginning of our . . . what to call it? Deterioration? Because the "hope and change" demagoguery came along, and the do-gooders (meaning self-inspired feel-gooders) fell for it, and the deterioration crept in, until its culmination right now. Also 2008 was two years before the more than five years that this home-bound New Life began. I can hardly recall what the old way of life felt like: freedom to sleep, freedom to write.

And then, finally:

July 14, 2015

Merrill, this note comes with neither a bang nor a whimper, but purely in the light of reality. It ought to have come sooner—I didn't realize that I had left some ambiguity. First, though, please know that I wish every imaginable blessing for health and joy and fulfilling productivity to you and all your beloveds, Joe and brilliant daughters and beautiful and gifted grandchildren, and that this wish will go on and on and on, without surcease, in all its truth and fervor. Still, our venerable correspondence has, as you must know, come to an end. We have already been divided for the last several years, I in sometimes furious frustration and you in a frequent sense of insult. I can no longer bear the frustration, and you, who have, I believe, taken the desire to engage for insult, hardly deserve to continue to feel offended. We live under different understandings.

> *Your* Weltanschauung *is not mine, and vice versa. We are not,*
> *as they say, on the same page. So let us turn the page to where it reads*
> *Finis, and bring an end to mutual irritation and despair.*
>   *Be well and happy, Cynthia*

No farewell speech could dissuade me from replying. I continued to write Cynthia, to remind her again that friends are not always on the same page. *"The focus of our correspondence,"* I wrote, *as
you required in recent years, has backed us both into a corner. The 'quotidian,' as you call it, has lost interest for you whereas it is still the center of my
world. You could no longer agree that it has any value up against the political
subjects that you are totally devoted to now."*

July 17, 2015

*Merrill, I am truly sorry that I may be causing you pain; I am neither
hard-hearted about the possibility nor oblivious to it . . . But if we were
to resume, we would instantly be back where we were, and to be there
is simply unsustainable. Case in point (though to bring this up is likely
to catapult us right into the abyss again): when you speak of "the political subjects that you are totally devoted to now" my heart sinks. Those
were "political" subjects? If that's how you categorize them, it's hopeless.
My last note to you was originally captioned "Day of Infamy." I finally
deleted those words, recognizing that you wouldn't have the slightest
insight into their meaning (vide the Book of Esther), though their meaning, and their intent, was on that very day scorching the earth. Cynthia*

Now she had clearly informed me that she considered me ig-
norant, and no longer worthy of her time, her friendship, or her
attention. Six months later, when I had my birthday on March 15
of 2017, I realized Cynthia would turn 89 on April 17. I found myself
writing to her once again:

April 17, 2017

Cynthia, I'm 79 years old, we are ten years, one month and two days apart. When you bid me goodbye, you wrote you could not in all honesty resume our "venerable correspondence." But you said "You will make something of it, I know. It is, after all, a Story. Or even a Novel."

What do you think of perhaps an Essay? After receiving your letter yesterday . . . I imagined—with a pounding heart—writing about our correspondence. Is it possible you would give me permission to quote from some of your letters to me?

Perhaps you could not. But I would have something new to live for and write about if you could allow it. Our lives were woven together for thirty-three years. Today I wish you Happy Birthday. Merrill

❋

April 17, 2017

Merrill, thank you for the birthday wishes! The number is daunting, and in my delusion I feel no relation to it. But the world judges by the impression it leaves. Mine the letters for whatever you wish. Even as an essay it will emerge as a story: your story. And your story will be the last word, since I can't conceive of ever writing about any of this. I don't have any autobiographical impulse at all. You write that "our lives were woven together." And wasn't that precisely the trouble? That they were not woven together? How many hundreds of times did I appeal to you to see how half of my obsessions never reached you at all, since in the nature of things you couldn't participate in them? But whoa (and woe): that last sentence is perilous, since it verges on the trouble starting up all over again. This, along with much else, was central to how we were NOT woven together. So stay well and happy and write freely!

❁

April 18, 2017

Cynthia,

In your address at the Ribalow Prize ceremony, you ask, "But what about the Jews? . . . Would I today want to argue with Merrill over whether her Jewish characters have conscious Jewish commitments, or promise what we like to call Jewish continuity? Never. I revise and chastise and regret my old acrid self."

Your criticism of me was evident at the first moment you reviewed my first book . . . and never changed. Nor was revised. I'm sorry you can't continue to love a person who loves you. You split with me most forcefully over a coming election, and how is it now, to have that illiterate and dangerous person as your president? Will he save Israel? He has divided the Jews in our country, creating hatred between the Orthodox and the other Jews. Whose spokesperson thinks there were "Holocaust Centers"? A man who can't speak a sentence, who Phillip Roth said has a vocabulary of 77 words. An idiot.

It's a bitter time, in our country, and in your heart. So my obsessions were not yours. We shared years of life, hundreds, perhaps thousands of hours of confidences. You do wish me well, thank you, but also you say a final goodbye and leave me with a broken heart.

Merrill

Letters Home From College: The Making of a Writer

FIRST LETTER HOME from college, February 1, 1956.

Dearest Mom, Daddy, and little sister, Bobbie,

My phone call must have cost a mint but I know you don't mind that I called. I think we talked about eight minutes. I feel all shivery. I've never been away from home so long—I do miss you all very much.

All my love, Merrill

In 1955, after graduating from Miami Beach High School, I went off to the University of Florida, in Gainesville—a pretty town located between Tallahassee on the west and Jacksonville on the east. Nearly every day of my four years there, I wrote letters home to my mother, who in turn typed letters to me from our family's apartment in Miami Beach. In 1962, this correspondence, carefully saved by my mother, crossed the country in an ancient truck my father bought to transport the contents of his antique store from Florida to California. On the nights that my mother and sister slept in a motel, my father kept watch on a blanket under the truck to protect his cargo. Now, in the late years of my life, I sit with the letters spread about me, discovering truths I had forgotten, all preserved in the written word.

Betty Lu Butterfield, my first roommate, was a blonde desperate to be chosen by a sorority, and who made fun of me as I steadfastly typed on my typewriter. She said things like: "Writing another poem, Merrill? Writing the great American novel, Merrill?" Betty Lu had six crinolines, all crammed into her side of the closet. Her bras were pink lace and padded, and her girdle was made of some kind of brown rubber. She played her Elvis records round the clock. When her friends were in the room, all of them smoking, they'd chatter till midnight, even when I begged them to leave. She was irritated that I already had a boyfriend and would ask, "Where do you and Joe go? Into the woods? Is that where you get all those mosquito bites? And what do you do in the woods with him?"

I did want to write a novel someday. The summer after high school I had worked posting mortgage payments in the offices of Marvin Lachmann Associates on Lincoln Road. Joe had a job in North Miami Beach posting stock market quotations on a blackboard in an investment office. My bus went south on Collins Avenue, Joe's bus north, and we timed our respective departures, each watching for the approaching bus and waving passionately as we sped past each other. His beautifully-formed forearm waving at me filled me with joy that had to last me for a long day of entering mortgage payments on a big green NCR machine. Other women in the office worked full-time for Mr. Lachmann, who always had a cigar in his mouth as he checked on our work. I dreaded the thought of growing up to be one of those secretaries, going into an office like his, taking dictation from a man like him, who always made a point of complimenting my dress or my hair in a way that disgusted me. "Aren't you a pretty little thing today!" he would say.

On my lunch hour I read, every day, a Shakespeare play. I knew I was college bound. Joe was also not going to be writing stock quotes on a blackboard all his life. I had met him the day before my 16th birthday at the meeting of a Young Judea club at Miami Beach High School. He was so handsome, already muscled and manly. He was, I knew as soon as we spoke, a deep soul. My heart leapt at the sight of him.

Both sets of our parents had moved to Miami Beach from Brooklyn, our fathers in search of some business venture that never worked out. Our mothers were both legal secretaries. Joe and I recognized each other as kindred spirits. Even at sixteen and seventeen we knew our destinies. Love. And college.

During the first meeting with my advisor at the University of Florida, she said, "With your interests, you will want to study with the great writing teacher here, Andrew Lytle. You may not take his class for credit freshman year, but he might let you sit in."

February 18, 1956

Dear Mom,

Just got your letter with the enclosure from "Seventeen" magazine, to which I'd sent a poem I wrote. I wish you had opened their letter. It's kind of silly for me to have to write you what it says. I am quite elated. It reads, "Dear Merrill, we're glad to tell you that your manuscript has passed our first reading and is being held for further consideration. You will hear from us again when a final decision is made. Be patient since this sometime takes a long time." I know it is only a maybe, but it's the first one I've gotten. You can open the second letter when it comes. Then send condolences and an aspirin if they say no.

❈

October 5, 1956

I have been reading the letters of Thomas Wolfe in a special dissertation that's kept in the library—although only grad students are supposed to be reading it. I wrote to Scribner's for permission, but my English professor arranged for the library to let me borrow it. I did get a reply from Scribner's. They wrote, "We don't feel we can release this manuscript. This seems a very unkind answer to your good letter which indicates that

*you are a young woman of quality and genuine interest in the field of lit-
erature." Little do they know I've already read most of it.*

*But Mom, when my letters are published, please be sure this one is
not included. I bet Thomas Wolfe was very careful about how he wrote.
This sure is a mess of grammar and mis-construed sentences and awful
typing and poor organization. The only thing I need to make me a good
writer is a new typewriter ribbon.*

❄

November 18, 1956

*The C-courses are really tough. Joe is helping me with astronomy, biol-
ogy, geography, geology, and history. My humanities professor today
informed me that the "A" grade on my essay test was largely due to
my originality, but on the objective test coming, I will have to know a
lot more facts to get an "A"—he doesn't believe it will be easy at all. It
is shocking to know how little I know about everything. All the time I
thought I was getting away with murder in high school I was really cheat-
ing myself. I feel like a complete moron sometimes.*

*Enclosed is a picture of my fella that his roommate took on the
porch. I think it is quite good. His slippers give the picture a perfect col-
legiate touch—you know, he just woke up or something.*

I am reading The Grapes of Wrath *again and can hardly get anything done it is so good.*

BY SOPHOMORE YEAR I had a new roommate, Mary Ella Fox from
Huntsville, Alabama. She was a hopeful education major, though
she complained bitterly about the idiotic courses she had to take in
her field. She and I got along well until I caught the Asian flu in the
epidemic of 1957 and had to be in the infirmary for a week with a
fever of 103. (The nurses were so short on medicine, you needed to
have a temperature of 104 before they would give you an aspirin.)
The entire gym was filled with cots for sick students. When I got

back to my room, Mary Ella had put her bed under one of two windows and her desk under the other one. We worked it out—I got to move my bed back under one of the windows. She turned out to be a good roommate, and she never minded my typing since she could sleep through it. We remained roommates through our junior year.

April 5, 1957

Thursday night I decided to sit in on Mr. Lytle's famous class. I ran all over trying to find where it was, and came in late, to HIS MAJESTY'S annoyance. There must have been twenty men there and one other woman. When I arrived so untimely, there was not another chair in the room and there was a major disruption when one of the men gave me his chair and started searching down the hall for another. In the final analysis, I don't think my arrival was appreciated by His Royal Civil War. His novel, The Velvet Horn, *has been on the best seller list for two weeks. Can't figure it out. I looked at it in the library. I wonder if I should buy the book ($3.95) and have him sign it and say something. It seems like a lot of money for a novel, but it might mean a lot to me later on when I'm through with school. What do you think?*

Truthfully, though, I enjoyed the class once I caught on to what they were discussing and will go every week if I have time. It lasted till after ten. Most of the men are married—a few aren't, but I know them, already.

❋

April 15, 1957

Andrew Lytle spoke to me today. Said he read the story I turned in and it was "pretty good." From him, that is something. Usually "not bad" is the farthest he goes. He says there are some things he wants to talk to me about—he first wants to read it in class. I suppose this is an honor, because he does it very rarely and when he does, he stops every minute to praise a word or phrase or sentence. I still do not like him. People I meet either hate or idolize him. I rather dislike him. Someone ought to tell him the Civil War is over. He concentrates on Southern literature, Southern writers, Southern decay, etc., till I am sick of it. I wonder how he can understand a story with a Northern setting written by a girl born in Brooklyn!

Mom and Daddy, after some hesitation, I am sending you the story I wrote. It is hard for you to see it objectively. I suppose I should have changed names to protect the innocent, but these names were the only ones that sounded right and I didn't expect anyone who knew the characters to read it. I hope you will not be offended, or think I am disrespectful to take things and twist them around to get the effect I desire. My memory gathers the facts together, and my write-ory organizes the facts into the most effective pattern. I realize the story may be unpleasant to read, and I promise you I meant nothing bad by the ending. My purpose in writing the story was not to portray an individual situation in reality but to depict the universal problems of the uselessness of old age and the loneliness, the memories.

I am told by a friend that the thought sequences of the old woman are quite believable. I have put my mind in the mind of the old woman and have taken the liberty of thinking for her. Probably Grandma does not resemble that old woman in any way. I do not know my grandmother, really—I only know who I think she might be, but can't be sure. If I'm wrong, I wonder what Grandma thought about all those years sitting at the window. I am beginning to feel bad again. When I wrote the story, I was almost crying—so removed I was from the present reality. Please try to understand what it is about. I don't want you to feel bad.

❖

April 17, 1957

Today has been a very productive day. I feel as if I have accomplished a great deal. I must have traveled five hundred miles on this typewriter and this is my last lap before calling it quits for a while.

I got inspired and wrote another story—seven pages in two hours— it just came flying out. By now you have read the story about Beckie and I hope that you have accepted it as something I wrote—no more, no less— I await your comments anxiously.

It is important for you both to realize that I draw from my experience, but embellish and change and exaggerate and underestimate so much that no one has any right to be offended or flattered or anything. The stories I think are best now are those far removed from me and college. Mostly about childhood. Thank God for my memory that remembers everything! About some things I amaze myself. I showed Joe my story after work tonight and for the first time in history he said "This is a beautiful story." He has never, never, never really liked anything I have done—this is truly an occasion.

OVER SPRING BREAK, after I turned nineteen, Joe and I decided to tell his parents that we were engaged. Their response was violent, both verbally and physically. In fact, his father cursed me and shoved me, trying to throw me down the stairs at the doorway of their apartment. The day before, because Joe could not afford to buy me a ring, we had "bought" one from my father, who was in the antique business and had a cigar box of odd rings at home. I picked one out—a little diamond ring for sixty dollars which Joe agreed to pay off at the rate of five dollars a month. My father didn't care if he never paid it off, but he wanted to smooth the way for us with Joe's parents.

April 25, 1957

I have stopped crying at last. I am still very much engaged, and I can't say exactly why I am not overjoyed at the fact. I am sorry I called you in tears the night we got back to school after his parents nearly killed me. When I got in, some girl noticed the ring and began screaming, "Merrill is engaged, oh, we must throw her in the shower." Somehow now I feel that if Joe had bought a ring worth three dollars for sixty dollars, it would be more valid than this. Of course, it was my fault because I wanted it, but now I am sorry. Not only did I come up to Gainesville to be with Joe, but my father sold him my engagement ring. It sounds rather awful.

Last night Joe's parents called him long distance and talked for over twenty minutes. They are still furious. The biggest mystery to me is why they are so strongly opposed. Joe says they feel I am not right for him, but does not know why they feel that way. I am a nice Jewish girl who does not smoke, drink, or gamble. I am not a tramp, I am polite at their house, I have good manners, I help with the dishes when she invites me over to dinner (and why did she ever invite me if she hates me so much?). If there are some unpleasant things about me, she has had no opportunity to see them as I am not really myself when I go there, anyway. If I were, I would have spit in her eye more than once. When Joe came home with all A's and showed her his report card, she said, "Hide that or your sister will be jealous." Not a word about what a great job he'd done, what a fine son he was.

I don't really know what the old bat thinks of me. Probably I am just not rich enough or beautiful enough for her son. If I were an ugly wretch it might be understandable why I was trying to (in her words) "tie Joe down," as if he were the only one I could "catch." I certainly have enough determination (if no other qualities) to catch another male very shortly, if given the chance. (As you know, there are lots of young men at school who are interested in me.) We surely did not set out to swindle their son. Neither am I pregnant, which she might think was the case. (Remember, just before I went to Gainesville, she said, to us both, "It's the girl's mother who's supposed to worry, but be careful anyway." What a thing to say!)

Joe says we at least can tell them that we will not get married until we can manage it financially. You can see this engagement is not the traditionally joyous one, and it is a little hard to beam ecstatically when someone says to us, "Oh, how wonderful." I have cried many tears. In fact, I'm taking off the ring, for good. I'll put it in my locked trunk and when we come home, we'll give it back to Daddy.

✿

November 17, 1957

Joe and I have got to earn some money. I've heard there is big money in writing—and I am determined to reap some benefits from the potboiler sort of stuff. Tell Daddy to think up some good confessional plots for me like "my heart was his playground," etc. They pay five cents a word and with a little effort and studying of the market I should be able to sell something. I am going to really try but I won't give up serious writing, of course.

✿

December 8, 1957

I was in the library with Joe last night, studying. I got up to go to the Ladies' Room. When I got back, Joe was gone from the table, with all his books. A friend of mine was also studying at our table and I asked him if he knew where Joe was. He replied that an older man who looked like Joe had come to the table and that Joe had got up and left with him. Can you believe he abandoned me? Much later he buzzed my room and said his father had taken him out to a steak dinner and then bought him a suede jacket. Of course, his father had come to bribe Joe to give me up. And of course, Joe had not told him we were studying together and that I would be back any minute. Joe is horrified by scenes, and no doubt he feared another huge blow-up. But he left me there and I can't believe he didn't stand up and tell his father the truth. I am sick of all this. Sick that we can't live our lives the way we choose to, and sad that Joe is so dependent on his parents to continue in college. Joe's mother wrote him a letter last week with a ten dollar check enclosed. He opened the envelope, handed it to me, and went to cash the check while I waited for him. I read the letter while he was inside the bank. "As we discussed, we hope you are not spending time with Merrill, since, as we told you, it is a very bad idea. Being as lazy as you are, you settled for the first thing that came along

Merrill and Joe in Miami Beach

when you could do much better. She is taking advantage of you, as you know. She is not for you! Don't let this go on! Get yourself out there and find some new girls to spend time with. She's not worth your time. You'll thank me for it. Love, Mother."

❁

December 15, 1957

At last I bought "The Velvet Horn," and Mr. Lytle signed it for me. I am thrilled to have it. He wrote: "To Merrill Joan Gerber, Who has great promise as an artist. Andrew Lytle, Christmas, 1957."

❁

March 10, 1958

Your Robert Frost clip arrived "a l'heure"—I opened your letter just after I got home from hearing him speak last night. Before we went, Joe gave me a book of his poems for my birthday, inscribing it: "For Merrill on her birthday—to make a poem out of the best parts." In fact, Robert Frost, in a shaky hand, signed the book for me after his reading.

Of course, he was very inspiring, very funny, and very old. I enjoyed it so much. Lytle was there with his daughter, Pamela, they had to sit on the balcony steps the house was so jammed. People were practically hanging from the chandeliers. All of Gainesville was there, and every-one from the university as well. Did you know Frost and his wife used to live in Gainesville and his wife died here? She died on March 20, 1938, five days after I was born. If I want to write a novel while I am still a teenager, I'd better get busy fast—five days left. Françoise Sagan wrote Bonjour Tristesse *when she was only eighteen.*

❊

April 18, 1958

Mr. Lytle read another story of mine in class last night. There were twenty-nine people there, the largest attendance since I have been going. Smith Kirkpatrick, by the way, found out yesterday that he was awarded one of the Sewanee Review *fellowships, which means he can stop teaching for a year and go somewhere to write. He is going to Mexico with his wife at the end of this semester. He is very happy about the whole thing.*

My story was a huge success. Lytle read it as though he were acting it on a stage. He enjoyed it as he read it because he looked up every few minutes as though to say, "See how she does it?" At one point he did say, "The dialogue is brilliant, don't you see?" Kirk said if I improved every six months as much as I have done in the last six, I will soon have not very far to improve to. Everyone knew without my saying that it was I who wrote the story, because everyone in the class was roused out of their usual lethargy to comment except me. It was great fun, there was a lot of laughter and everyone looked at me with respect. I suppose that this is one of the few times that I am ever in the spotlight, and it means more to me than I can ever tell anyone. No one ever looks at me with respect any other time, and I know I am good in some way. In my stories I can say, "See? This is me! This is what I can do!" and finally they believe it. But it is a pallid glory because when class is over, I just go home, and that is all. It is now that I am reassured and I want to write again urgently.

This morning I saw Lytle on campus and he said he wanted to talk to me and will, next week. Measles are going around school now and he looked as if he had caught it, but of course I did not say anything. I don't think he normally has little red dots all over his face!

❋

May 3, 1958

I spoke to Mr. Lytle this afternoon for a long time and for the first time he was actually friendly, nice! He said I have taken great strides and have real professional skill but does not know if it can continue at the rate of speed it is at now. He recommends living in New York for me but says no one knows where the right place to be is or the right thing to do. He has done so much himself and is still not satisfied, etc. He thinks I should write regularly every day especially during the summer, when there is a tendency to stagnate, and read for stimulation when I feel stale, and adopt two or three great writers to copy from and absorb. "If you keep writing, you will finally find what your intention is and what subject matter you will ultimately want to be yours." Talking to him is wonderful.

❋

May 16, 1958

Last Sunday I wrote another story, based on my earlier version but expressed differently, rewritten in location, dialogue etc.—only the characters stayed the same. I gave it to Lytle and expected him to glance at it and comment briefly because I did not feel it was too good. Instead, he read it in class last night, the last class of the semester. The consensus was that although the other one was good the new one is better. Lytle said, "This is a mighty good story—comes close to a story that will sell if it isn't already there."

He wants me to think about a few minor points and talk to him and then send it off, perhaps to the New Yorker. *Lytle intends to write a letter to go along with it. He said he does not do this often because his reputation is too important to do it with every story that comes along. I have been stopped on the street all day today with comments like "I heard you wrote a very fine story and Lytle can't believe you've come so far.*" Smith Kirkpatrick, who teaches with Lytle, stopped me in the cafeteria this afternoon and said "You ought to be mighty proud of that story. That's fine writing. You don't find writing as good as that in many magazines these days." Needless to say I am very pleased but I'm going slow and will not get hysterical and lose perspective right now. I feel as if I will never be able to write another good story but I always feel that way so it doesn't worry me too much.

I know Lytle is extremely pleased because he cringes from the thought of "selling" unless the artistic side is taken care of and only then, he says, we worry about the finances. The Florida Review will be out Monday with my story "The People in China," in it—and I will send it to you right away. I am still reworking the new one so it will be a while. I am more and more convinced that my writing is not a hobby and although I don't think either you or Daddy really take me seriously, no one really knows how seriously I take myself and have since I was a very small child. I don't know what I will do when I graduate but I don't think I can stop writing and be happy teaching somewhere without doing the thing most important to me—my writing.

❁

May 18, 1958

We had another riot and attempted panty raid last night, and this campus is really getting violent. Twenty-three boys were arrested and a policeman is in the hospital in critical condition because they attacked him when he tried to break up the riot. It stems from the beer crackdown, I think. We all locked our doors, shut the lights, and stayed in our rooms. Those things are no longer fun when they reach a wild intensity.

❀

May 23, 1958

Today is the very last day of classes, and I am sorry to see this semester end. I might even decide, last minute, to come to summer school if I cannot get a good job or if the summer looks too rough in other ways (that is if Joe has to be at home controlled by his mother and her plans for him). Yesterday, my drama teacher from last year, Dr. Stryker, stopped me on the street to show me he was carrying a term paper I wrote for his class on Arthur Miller. He was going to read it in his class; he felt that since my name was currently in circulation in "The Florida Review," and that in my paper I mentioned a desire to write, it would be apropos to read it in his class.

Smith Kirkpatrick told me that Andrew Lytle left yesterday for New York, taking with him my story. *Here is a more accurate description of what he plans to do with it: show it to the publishers of his book,* The Velvet Horn—*McDowell, Obolensky—and since they know the publishing world "inside out," have them suggest a market and perhaps have them submit it directly to that market. Or maybe Lytle will take it directly to the* New Yorker, *himself. Still pretty wonderful, any way you look at it.*

❀

May 25, 1958

Lytle is probably back by now and I would love to call him, but will wait till tomorrow. Probably, as I have said, he just left my story in the bottom of his suitcase and forgot all about it. I am prepared for anything. Or everything.

❁

May 26, 1958

As I said, I was prepared for anything. Lytle told me this morning that whoever it was he was supposed to show my story to was out of town or on a publishers' convention and therefore could not read my story. Lytle spoke to him long-distance, but did not see him. But I do know that my story is back here in Gainesville, unread and unnoticed.

Lytle told me he was really sorry and disappointed (what about me?) and it was just a bad break. But he wants me to send the story off myself, and let it speak for itself.

So I will. Actually, this is not tragic, only a little unfortunate.

❁

June 21, 1958

Last night I took a book out of the library that impressed me so much, I stayed up half the night reading it. Probably, had I been a little younger I would have tried to pattern the rest of my life after the girl in the book. This letter is especially for my sister, Bobbie.

The name of the book is The Diary of a Young Girl *by Anne Frank. It is a true story; a real diary written by a thirteen-year-old Jewish girl during the war. It was written at a time when all the Germans were killing the Jews. She and her family—mother, father, and older sister—had to hide in a big deserted office building for two years so they would not be caught and tortured by the Germans. Her thoughts are so typical (at least of many of mine when I was thirteen) that you feel you are her good friend as you read the book. She feels no one understands her, that they pick on her unfairly, that they do not see her as a real, complete person, but as a silly child. Eight people hide in this building for two years, never once leaving it to go outside. In the other family there is a fourteen-year-old boy whom Anne falls in love with as they get to know each other better and better. You can imagine how little there is to do when you are practically in prison for two years—everyone gets on everyone's nerves and they fight and quarrel all the time. They cannot even look out the window in the daytime, and are constantly afraid the German police will find them. To help pass the time, Anne starts a diary in which she puts down all of her thoughts. She calls the diary "Kitty" and always starts her entries: "Dear Kitty" to sound like a letter. They have food and books smuggled in. Anne tries to keep up with her lessons. Bombs are always falling outside and they are frightened and horrified that they will be taken prisoners.*

Dear sister of mine, if you read it, you will probably want to start a diary the same day. Please try to read it, Bobbie, I know you will enjoy this and it really might inspire you. It is a very famous and important book, especially for the Jews. And I won't tell you how it ends either.

In 1958, when I was twenty years old, my maternal grandmother died in Brooklyn at the age of eighty-seven. My grandfather had bought the Brooklyn house for $9,999 in 1925. I lived there with my family till I was fourteen, when we moved to Miami Beach. My aunt and grandmother continued to live there till my grandmother died, after which my mother and aunt sold the house.

July 24, 1958

I suppose I have written my last letter to 405 Avenue O, and this makes me feel very sad. If we had tons of money, I would have liked us to keep the house forever. I am sure that if we ever looked under the lilac tree or the wishbone tree, we would find great big roots assigned to Jessie, William, Merrill and Barbara. Also to Greta and Gram and Spotty and various turtles, fish and cats.

It is terrible to feel so familiar with the house, to know the cracks in the tiles, and the stairs that squeak, the pipes under the sink, and the water gauge in the oil burner, and then lose it. I know this is unforgivably sentimental but I feel some homage must be paid our home. The hardest part will be going back someday and finding strange people there.

When they put in new flooring, they will find fifteen-year-old lima beans wrapped carefully in a paper napkin which I deposited there through a hole in the floor. I don't care what the deed says. Papers don't make something belong to someone. It will always be our house.

On another subject, I met a professor here last night, Pedro Villa Fernandez, who shared an office with Thomas Wolfe at NYU many years ago. He had coffee with him at ten-thirty every morning. Wolfe looked like he had slept on a park bench every night. Big, awkward, creased, sloppy, lazy, ponderous. The professor said if he'd known Wolfe would ever become famous, he would have indulged in some hero worship.

He nearly died of shock when Wolfe came tearing in one day to say he had had a novel accepted. Wolfe hated to teach, threw away half his papers and told the students they were so bad he couldn't bear to grade them. He would get to class ten minutes late every day on the fifth floor of NYU and hope the class had left because he hated to teach them. Not a very admirable guy, but it depends how you look at it. I love his writing. Like from Of Time and the River—"to wreak . . . the rude and painful substance of his own experience into the . . . blazing and enchanted images that are themselves the core of life." *You know, he died in 1938, six months to the day after I was born. I think I was meant to replace him.*

BY THE FIRST HALF of senior year, I was living alone in the basement of Broward Hall in a room shaped like a triangle. Of course, I did not want to live in the dorms at all, I wanted to live with Joe, but this was impossible and would be for some time. At least in a single room there was freedom from roommates—if not freedom from noise—since my window overlooked the back patio of Broward where weekend dances were often held till curfew. I bought a black metal fan that created a low hum, aimed it at the wall and fell asleep while it purred and sighed. The joy of privacy, the liberty to type night and day, was ecstasy for me. I had been awarded the Typing Medal in high school (not the English Medal I desired), but I discovered that typing was a great joy to me. I began recording my dreams as soon as I awoke. With my eyes closed, I was able to recreate the setting, the people around me, the ambience, the emotions. It was a perfect writing exercise: the dream-adventure flowed effortlessly from my fingers. I didn't have to create plot or purpose or meaning—the dream made itself into the story.

September 26, 1958

Yesterday morning Lytle asked me to bring to class "what I had done last summer"—so he could read it, sight unseen. Well, I had done nothing of consequence over the summer so I went home and in less than two hours wrote a story called "A Final Note." The paper was still warm by class time. Lytle was really taking a chance, reading something he had not read before in front of a new and record-size class.

He read the pages kind of fast and sloppy, as though he didn't like the story, and I thought the end had come. Only he did like it, and he and the students talked about it for longer than it took me to write it. The old grand piano in the story got kicked around as a symbol for two hours. Did you know that a piano in a family can mean a sign of cultural straining? An object of inheritance? A sign of vanity? A sign of a permanent home, for they were not made to be carried around from place to place? A sign of unity (group singing)? I always learn so much about what I mean in that class! I have an appointment with Lytle this afternoon to discuss it further. No one must ever know how fast I wrote it.

※

November 5, 1958

Last night was Lytle's class, which went very well. He smiled at me when I came in. He read Flannery O'Connor's story, "A Good Man is Hard to Find." He read it like an actor (which he is), his eyes sparkling at some parts, and his demeanor grim at others, especially when the murders are taking place. When he finished, there was silence in the room. He turned to me. "Would you like to elucidate?" I did my best, trying to ex-

plain what I thought he was looking for. Symbols, enveloping action, action proper, terms he always uses. When I was through, he said, "You have done a brilliant job of everything there. Now, what is the ultimate meaning of it all?" This time it was probably the realization of a wasted life, or hubris or humiliation, or the fatal flaw or original sin, or something biblical. He sometimes says, "Follow the thread into the labyrinth and there you will find the answer." Or, "Immerse yourself in the destructive element and let the deep, deep water bear you up." I never know what Lytle means for sure, he has an air of mystery about him all the time. He always seems to know what a story's dark secrets are. But he said I did a good job, in any case.

JUST BEFORE THE SECOND SEMESTER of senior year, I learned of a room for rent in a house on NW 15th Street, just north of Anderson Hall, where most of my classes were held. I walked up a tree-lined street that seemed almost like a country road, smelling of winter leaves and freedom. A young woman named Jane Hunter met me on the front porch. Through the screen door I could see a large colored woman inside the house—as she passed the door, she flashed a smile at me. "Hello honey," she said, cracking the door. "You sure could use a little meat on your bones."

"This is Willie Mae," Jane said. "She takes care of all of us and bakes the best biscuits you ever tasted."

Jane led me into the room for rent, a big wooden-walled space with a window looking out to the street. There were two beds in the room, two closets, a carved dresser with many drawers, and a small private bathroom with a tiny stall shower. This room and the opposite room at the back of the house, Jane explained, were both heated by a kerosene stove in between, which kept everyone cozy in the winter. She sat down on one of the beds and invited me to sit on the other. She confided that this was her first time renting a room to a student; her parents had been killed six months ago in a car accident. She and her sister lived in one bedroom at the other end of the house and their ninety-three-year-old grandmother, stroke-ridden, lived in the other. Willie Mae took care of everyone.

Jane also told me that she was a teacher at P. K. Yonge Elementary School and her younger sister was in high school. They were renting out these two rooms to students because they needed the money. Rent would be thirty dollars a month.

"I love it—I'll take it," I said. "I'll move in as soon as I can."

At last, I felt like an adult, in charge of my space and time.

January 25, 1959

I got a rejection, finally, after six weeks, from Esquire. *"I liked your story 'Peter, Peter, Pumpkin Eater' very much, good handling, treatment, etc., but too sentimental. Am very interested in seeing other mss of yours." Signed Gene Lichtenstein, (whoever he is).*

❖

March 12, 1959

I am at the point now where I put on six different items of clothing before I leave the house in the morning because I am so tired of everything I own. I asked Idella, the colored girl who also works for the Hunters, if she had some extra time to do some ironing for me because I can't find a place in my room to set up an ironing board and because I don't like to iron. She said she would and I started taking out my few things. Would you believe it—I counted twenty-four blouses never ironed and I've been wearing them all winter. She looked at the pile and said it would cost about $1.25 which is absolutely fine with me. They would take me about fifteen hours to do. Jane Hunter pays her fifty cents an hour which is awfully cheap I think. Idella is my age. She should be in college like I am.

❊

April 6, 1959

I went over to Mr. Lytle's yesterday and visited him for most of the afternoon.

We didn't do much. Lytle was not feeling well—he has been traveling a lot, drinking and smoking a lot, and getting very little sleep. It is telling. This is the price he pays for being who he is. When Lytle drove me home, we gossiped about everyone in the class and talked about things that were fun. It is so nice to have a "family" to visit in Gainesville. When he told me that he was going to a party that night and didn't much look forward to it, I asked him if I could baby-sit Langdon. At 7 p.m., Lytle brought Langdon over to the dorms and she stayed with me all evening. Langdon is terribly spoiled but it is hard to ignore her precocity at age five and her loveliness. I have a standing invitation to come to Lytle's house and visit.

Lytle is so warm and generous and so personal with me; he is tremendously different from the man I thought he was when I first met him. I am very glad I came here to study with him—he has worked wonders with my mind, some of which have not even appeared yet. They will take a long time to get to the surface or shall I say a long time to get below the surface.

❊

April 11, 1959

I am getting increasingly impatient with school. Sometimes, when I am analyzing the accents in a line of poetry, or discussing with great seriousness the image of an eagle in one of Shelley's poems, I get the terrible feeling that this is all so "on the fringes" of real things, that people go out and farm and work and sweat to earn their living, and I am pettily employed with versification and imagery and rhyme schemes.

❄

April 15, 1959

New developments. Andrew Nelson Lytle won a Guggenheim fellowship, which means he is going to Peru and Mexico next February, which may mean that if I stay here I will not be able to get my Master's Degree (by June) unless I am able to complete my thesis before Lytle leaves in February, all things being allowed.

Next, I've learned that half the English staff is interceding about getting me a fellowship, the verdict being uncertain. Lytle said he will see Rothschild this summer and see if he can get $1000 for me. My friend, the poet Barry Spacks, is writing (his idea) to his creative writing professor at Indiana to see if any assistantships are still available there. Everyone is helping, even strangers. I have a lot of friends here.

I had dinner last night with a woman, a very fine grad student who is married to a med student. She noticed that my eyes do not function together and is almost sure that if the muscles were clipped, I would learn to see things out of both eyes at the same time. She was very interested in my being Jewish. This is not a well-known fact, but she said that because the Jews are a small group and have been interbreeding for thousands of years, we are somewhat like royalty and defective genes tend to become more evident as we become a closer inbred group. It is very interesting that some diseases are peculiar almost only to Jews. Diabetes is more common among Jews than any other group. Even Jewish doctors who know this do not discuss it because it has always been ideal for Jews to marry Jews, even among doctors, but eugenically, it would be more ideal to marry out of this ethnic group. That will not be my choice however, despite the efforts of Joe's parents to separate us. They never will.

IN 1959, I ENTERED the Mademoiselle College Fiction Contest, which was open to all undergraduate girls. I was one of two Honorable Mentions; the winner was Joyce Carol Oates. This is the note I received.

April 24, 1959

Dear Miss Gerber,

Congratulations! If you fulfill all the requirements for Mademoiselle's college fiction contest you have been chosen to receive one of the honorable mentions. Will you send us a recent photograph and some biographical information, and a statement to the effect that you come within all the regulations of the contest. Since we will give out releases in connection with our August issue we would appreciate if you would not make public announcements till then. Looking forward to hearing from you with all good wishes,

Margarita G. Smith, fiction editor

❉

April 29, 1959

The Mademoiselle contest is a famous contest and it's pretty nice to be one of four in the nation chosen as a winner. They may even buy one of the stories. I think it is my biggest success so far. When I got the letter, I ran all the way to Lytle's office and he was pleased as could be. He went around telling more people than I did.

❉

May 3, 1959

I went to the Gainesville library Friday afternoon and looked through some back issues of Mademoiselle. In the August issues all they do is publish the pictures of the winners but only the names of the honorable mentions. So all that trouble with sending them a picture is only just in case they ever publish your work. But I also looked to see if any of the honorable mentions were ever published later and the answer seems "Nay." I guess all the good to come out of this has already come.

❊

May 30, 1959

Went over to see Mr. Lytle today—he really is in pretty bad shape; he looks about ninety years old. During an exploratory exam he went into shock and if his wife Edna had not noticed it he would've possibly not been alive anymore. This local doctor who did the exam said that an operation is necessary within two weeks or his bladder may collapse. It looks pretty serious and scary. Of course, he will not be able to teach at Harvard this summer or go to see his daughter Pamela graduate from high school up at Sewanee, Tennessee. He may not even be able to utilize his Guggenheim. Mrs. Lytle feels that they should get another opinion from a big clinic, possibly in Tennessee, before they go ahead with this major surgery. She would not know what to do with the children if she and Lytle flew to Tennessee. I offered to stay with them if it is really necessary that they go. But they would have to be away for a long time and would have to take the children with them. Being there in their house, in these circumstances, was a terrible visit, with their old dog Cory on his last legs and dying. He is not a cheerful thing to see dragging around the house.

Lytle is taking this fairly badly—he loves life and he is surprised by all this and annoyed more than anything. He is so honest. He said that it was fairly pleasant going into shock, probably like dying, which shows that he has been thinking about death. He wants me to come over before I leave for home to talk about an ending change on one of my "Crazy Harry" stories. I don't care at all about stories now but he seems to want to think about other things besides himself.

THE FOLLOWING is the first of seventy-one letters Andrew Lytle wrote to me.

September 1, 1959

Dear Merrill,

Let me set you at rest at once about my teaching here this fall . . . I am mending faster now. The sorrows you've had with your writing this summer may be that inward struggle which will bring you out of the stalemate of your previous subject. Of course it may not. It may mean you will not be a writer. Only you can tell this. If you can't leave it alone, then you've got to struggle with it. And you may come into your own. You will, I believe, if you keep at it.

It won't be long before you return. I'll be looking forward to seeing you. Langdon is growing and changing mighty fast. First grade tomorrow.

As ever, ANL

After I graduated with honors from the University of Florida, I received a scholarship to get my MA at Brandeis University, where Joe was already doing his graduate work. Around that time, my mother wrote Andrew Lytle a thank-you note for what she felt he had done for me. He replied:

October 22, 1959

Dear Mr. and Mrs. Gerber,

You were very kind to write me such an encouraging note. Of course, such a response from so gifted and intelligent and interesting a person as your daughter makes the teacher feel good. One of the sad things about my secondary profession is that the students always go away. I hope she does well where she is. As a matter of fact, I think I have taught her all I can. She needs to be on her own now and push herself and see what she can do. Thank you both for your letter. It is very moving.

Sincerely, Andrew Lytle

Shortly before Joe and I were married on June 23, 1960, Lytle wrote me the following:

May 2, 1960

Dear Merrill,

I hope for you all the happiness and well-being in this marriage. You have hinted at impediments which you've now overcome. But you will also need vigilance if it is his mother. Once you are joined together, all the odds are on your side.

I don't know whether I met your affianced to know him, but he is a lucky boy. Why don't you make him support you? Nothing could be better for him with one hundred dollars coming in now and then from your work.

Affectionate regards—in haste—ANL

Merrill with Andrew Lytle (left) and Smith Kirkpatrick at an event honoring Andrew Lytle, De Kalb College, Georgia, 1989.

Andrew Lytle died December 12, 1995 at the age of ninety-two. He and I corresponded for thirty-five years. I visited him at the Log Cabin in Monteagle, Tennessee at the end of his life. His daughter Lilly Langdon and I also wrote to each other, and still do:

October 18, 2016

Dear Langdon,

Yesterday I opened a huge box of letters marked "Letters Home from College" and began reading the hundreds of letters I'd written my mother and father from UF. I came across this letter written in your house while I baby-sat you on Friday, October 3, 1958, 58 years ago! I loved you so much as I read it, and loved your father and mother, and your dog and your sisters, that I have to send it to you. They've all come alive for me again, though it breaks my heart. Of course my parents are long dead as well, and I—I am seventy-eight years old. In fact, Joe and I have been married fifty-six years. We have three daughters and five grandchildren.

I never did give up writing, as your father feared I might, and this month, breast cancer awareness month, I am publishing my thirtieth book, a memoir titled Beauty and the Breast, A Tale of Breast Cancer, Love and Friendship.

Life is risky when you get old (I have just had a knee replacement, eight weeks ago, and am very slowly recovering from it). Please tell me how you are, what you're doing, how things are working out. I am finding in these letters many details about my writing class with your father, his illnesses and his great and tragic losses. How brutal that your mother died of cancer when you were only nine, and your sister Kate also died young of it and left two young children.

Sitting here among these letters, I am reliving my college years again, with so much ahead of me then, all of life in front of me, adventures, the hope of being a writer, love, marriage, children. Now there is so much less ahead—I find it easy to cry.

I so wish we had been able to publish the book of letters written between Andrew and me, and between him and another student, my friend, Jack De Bellis. We called it, Andrew Lytle's Correspondence with Two Students. *Your father wrote me seventy-one letters, and I wrote him more than one hundred. We sent the manuscript to many publishers, but they all refused it. You know I visited your father in the log cabin in Monteagle when he was very old.*

Eventually my papers (and his) may be in Yale Library—I've been told Yale is interested in seeing my archive later this year. So darling girl, send news, send a picture, and know I send you much love—now see the letter below that I wrote home to my parents from your house so long ago.

❋

October 3, 1958

Dearest Family, I am writing to you from Andrew Lytle's living room. It is almost eleven p.m. It is quiet here except for the crackling of a few crickets and it is cool and lovely. Lilly Langdon is fast asleep in her bed. She is the most wonderful little girl I have ever met, with all the wisdom of the ages in her little head.

The Lytles have gone to a wedding tonight, their seventeen-year-old daughter Pamela is away at school, their twelve-year-old girl Kate is at a party, and I am baby-sitting Lilly Langdon. Mr. Lytle asked me in the library this afternoon if I would mind staying with his little one for a while. On the way over to his house, Mr. Lytle introduced me to a friend of his in the car as "a prospective writer."

"She's good," he said, "but when she first got here, she came arrogantly into the class and didn't think I was any good—isn't that right?" he asked me. I was rather thunderstruck. My friend, Jack De Bellis, had told him how I felt in the beginning and so I had to admit my initial dislike. But I also assured him of my current admiration for him and we are fine friends again. Earlier today, before all this, he wanted to discuss

my graduate work. He said I am at a delicate point in my development and must fight to keep writing for it is at this point that one continues or stops.

He said, "I would like to have you stay here but I think that per-haps by now you have learned as much from me as you can and should look at things from a new point of view." Still, he said he will talk to the proper authorities about getting me an assistantship. His wife, Edna, was wearing a beautiful red dress tonight and when I admired it, she smiled at me and said, "When you turn forty, you either buy a red dress or take a lover." I understand that great people can be tired and be sus-ceptible to many ills. This house is full of old furniture and dignity but life is everywhere.

The Lytles came home, now I am back at the dorm. I had a really fine evening and would love to be a permanent member of that family for a while. One could learn a lot from the way Mr. Lytle conducts his family. If I can ever remember all the things I heard tonight I'll tell you about them. It would take me a hundred pages now. When I asked Lang-don if she would be a student in her father's class when she grows up she said simply, "He'll be dead then."

The teenage sister came home from the dance about 11:30, all tired out. She is very pretty. She had a glass of milk and went to bed. The Lytles have an eleven-year-old dog who cannot come into the house because he became infested with ticks, millions of them. Now they bathe the dog every week but still have to keep him outside. Most of the time Lytle gets up at five in the morning to work and they are all in bed by eight. I can't begin to tell you how enthused I am about finding humanity in genius.

At the DMV

A T THE DMV, seated on a green plastic chair, an African-American woman is using her smart phone as a mirror as she applies mascara to her eyelashes. Next to her a teenaged Asian-American girl, wearing mini-shorts and sandals, keeps her head down, her black hair falling over her face, as she checks her phone. A young Hispanic couple come rushing in the "Appoint-ments Only" door—the woman holding a baby and the man looking baffled as to where to go or what to do next. Against the side wall are the restroom doors—a single restroom for each sex, and seven or eight people waiting on line to get into each, in a building that at this moment holds what seems at least a hundred people. I have been in the women's rest room: there is no hook for a purse and the floor is always wet.

My husband sits in the front row of chairs, waiting with others to be summoned for an 8:15 AM drive-test and I sit in the row behind him. Twelve years ago, a macular hole appeared in his right eye and he had surgery to close it. As a result, the DMV has required him to take a behind-the-wheel driving test every year. Though his eye has been stable, and each year the required eye exam attests to it, the drive-test is required. I always accompany him to the DMV and I always wait here for him. I wear my shabbiest clothes and oldest shoes. As soon as I get home I shed and toss into the trash everything I wear in this environment.

When they call my husband's name, I go up to Window 22 with him. Of the two women at the desk, one, a black woman, wears a knitted cap low over her forehead, almost over her eyebrows. She is dressed in a gray t-shirt with a stretched-out neck. The woman beside her has breasts that are falling out of her blouse. In wonderment, my eyes cleave to her cleavage.

"Your license, your insurance, your car registration," the black woman says and holds out her palm. My husband, whose hand is shaking slightly, hands her the papers. She studies them. "Your current eye exam." He offers her the two-page document he got last month from the ophthalmologist. She glances at it and hands it back. "You need a *current* eye exam; this one is from last year."

"No," I interject. "This exam was done last month! See the date?"

The woman takes the papers from my husband's hand and shoves them toward me. The date on it is last year's date, not this year's.

"It's a mistake! The doctor obviously made a mistake; we were just there last month."

"Sorry," the woman says, "We can't accept this."

"But we have a drive-test appointment. We had to wait months to get it. I swear my husband had his eye exam last month. I was there with him." I am, to my surprise, close to tears, swearing to this woman in the crazy knitted hat that now seems to be down over her eyes.

The young woman with the breasts is listening in. "Can you contact the doctor and have him fax us a corrected exam?"

"I don't know! I could try!"

The scheduled hour of my husband's precious drive exam is slipping away. The woman hands me a slip of paper. "This is the fax number here." I don't know how I will achieve this task. I dig my cell phone out of my purse. The noise in the DMV is rising around my ears like a tsunami wave. My husband sits down, his head bowed.

"I'll see what I can do." I go outside where the sun is blinding, where some guy is smoking, though it is forbidden at the DMV. I begin the impossible: calling the HMO, asking for the eye exam department, asking the receptionist there if she can solve this dilemma. "Help me," I say to her. "We are lost at sea. We are at the DMV and my husband can't take his driving exam without his eye exam and Dr. So and So (your imbecile doctor, I am thinking) signed the wrong date at the bottom of the form and we are desperate."

"The doctor is with a patient. I can't speak to him till he finishes the exam." I give her my cell phone number and the fax number at the DMV.

"Please call me back as soon as he sends a fax," I beg her.

I tell my husband what I have done. His hands are visibly shaking. We are so stressed that I now see this ordinary movement of his in a different, more sinister, light. My husband has what is called an "essential tremor"—not a disease, not Parkinson's, not progressive, in fact it's genetic, his mother had it. (And therefore, our children could one day have it. I am horrified, suddenly, at this dangerous inherited possibility. It's his mother's fault. So much of what is wrong with him is his mother's fault. And she, who hated me till the day she died, lives on as one quarter of each of my children).

What further horrifies me is how we could have gotten to be such old people. My husband's birthday is tomorrow, on which date his driver's license will expire. In the DMV we see dozens of young people of various races, all here to continue their wild and fortunate lives of driving cars to places where they will do their sexy, healthy, exciting stuff and then there are just a few old folks, like us, whose freedoms could be snatched away in a second.

There are warning signs on the walls of the DMV declaring that threatening an employee will lead to an arrest and court date and a fine and conviction with prison time. Also that it is illegal to bring firearms into the DMV. People in front of various windows here are arguing with people behind the windows. There is a level of anger in this building that is palpable. At the least there should be more than one restroom per sex.

The endless drone of the loudspeaker bombards us. "Now serving G003 at Window Number 6. Now serving B013 at Window Number 11."

I'm holding my cell phone in my hand. More than a half hour has passed since the scheduled drive-test appointment. A half hour later, I go outside and call the receptionist at the eye-doctor's again. No progress has been made; he is still with a patient. We sit and we stare aimlessly forward. If I were home, I could be playing Spider Solitaire on my computer; I could be eating the one leftover donut in the box on the kitchen table.

So many young and handsome people pass before my eyes. In their short skirts, the girls have perfect thighs and adorable knees, the guys in their white undershirts are macho, sexy, powerful looking, many with mustaches. There is an incredible aura of sex in this room.

My phone vibrates. I run outside so I can hear who is calling. The receptionist informs me that the doctor has sent a fax. I rush to tell the woman with the hat that the fax has been sent. She leaves her desk. I indicate to my husband by hand motions that some progress is taking place. The woman comes back and shows me a note scribbled and signed by the eye doctor: *"Sir, the exam was this year. I indicated the wrong year."*

"We can't accept this note," the woman tells me. "He has to fax us a new, complete, eye exam form, filled out."

"What? The doctor faxed a correction. He *signed* it."

"Sorry, you'll have to get a new completed exam form signed." She lays the note on her desk. "I'm on break now," she says and walks away. The woman with the breasts (and so soft and comforting they now look to me) says, with pity: "Maybe our manager will approve this letter anyway. I'll be right back." And she rushes away with the paper. I turn toward my husband who is watching me from his chair. There are times that time stands still and this is one of them. The breasts come back toward me. "I got it approved," she says, smiling. "Your husband can take his driving test. Have him bring his car around the side of the building, and put these papers on your dashboard."

"Thank you, thank you," I can't thank her enough, this angel who has managed to free us from these hard chairs. As we go out of the building, I see again the same black woman I saw earlier continuing to apply mascara to her eyelashes. How beautiful, exactly, does she, does anyone, need to be at the DMV?

The inside of the car is hot; this is the end of July in California. My husband drives the car around the building and gets on line for the drive-exam. His hands are trembling. Two cars are ahead of him. Waiting on a concrete bench nearby are parents or a buddy of a hopeful driver, each waiting for the car, with his person in it, to come back with the examiner. Their anxiety, if they have any, is invisible. Those with phones are texting away, or talking, or taking selfies. A guy in ragged jeans, wearing a helmet and a leather jacket, is sitting in full sun. A tattooed girl in a halter top, her back and arms covered with snakes, is applying lipstick to her pierced lips. If I hadn't married my husband so long ago, I wouldn't be in this hell now. There were so many young men who admired me in college. My life could have gone in any direction but this one.

Ahead I see a kind-looking female examiner with her clipboard introducing herself to the driver of the car at the starting line. She looks human, almost sympathetic, if only my husband could get her! But off she goes, and the next examiner comes to the car ahead. He looks Chinese. We watch the routine: brake lights, turn signals, hand signals, horn honking, and then the man gets into that car. Now it is our turn.

We move up slowly to the white line. A man comes toward our car and my gut clenches. He has a sour, fierce, dark, ugly face. He says to me through my husband's open window, "Exit the car now." This man is a Nazi. I grab my purse and get out, and go to the trunk to retrieve a folding chair I brought along for this very purpose. The man is speaking in harsh tones to my husband as he goes through his commands and then he gets into the car. Oh God, we are doomed.

I drag my chair to where there is a drop of shade in the waiting area. My husband is apparently listening to the man's instructions. He releases the brake and drives slowly forward. Then he is gone.

The book I brought to entertain myself during this time is called "A Widow's Story," and is a memoir by a woman, my age, whose husband dies unexpectedly and her life is destroyed in the blink of an eye. This of course is my ultimate nightmare, the terror that my husband will die and leave me abandoned. In any case, one of us will surely lose the other. Several of the women I know are widows and have survived the brutal job of taking care of a dying husband (some for months and some, unimaginably, for years).

The author of the memoir, though nearly insane with grief and terror, has many friends who support her, and who send her "grief baskets." Deliveries of food arrive, health-fruit drinks and cheeses and huge pears and sausages; also potted plants and even trees. I take account of my friends, not so many after all, and realize none would send me so much as a banana.

I sit outside of the DMV reading, checking my watch from time to time: where is he now, what critical mistakes is he making? So much as bumping a curb will end the test. No matter how rotten and afraid I feel now, no matter how I fear that my husband will lose his license and we will both be shunted directly into an old age home, nothing I feel is as bad as the terror the widow feels in the book I am reading. She can't eat. She can't sleep. She imagines hideous basilisks beckoning her to die.

I close the book. Why didn't I just bring along a *New Yorker* or a crossword puzzle? There is something wrong with me that I am so willing to jump into suffering with the pure certainty that I deserve it. I knew this since I was a little girl. Life will end badly, incredible pain will be my lot, I will be left alone and bereft.

A familiar form materializes in front of me. What? My husband is back, how can that be, it's too soon. The Nazi is walking ahead of him to the door of the DMV and my husband says to him, "Will you tell my wife what you told me?" The Nazi looks at me with disgust. "Your husband has a severe, dangerous tremor, he should not be on the road, I am going to recommend that his license be revoked, I will report him to the Safety Division."

He goes in the door and shuts it in my husband's face. "What did you do wrong?" I accuse him.

"He said I drove not up to speed on Orange Grove. He said my hands were shaking."

"Did you tell him you don't have a disease? That you've had a perfect driving record for sixty years?" I look at my beautiful, handsome, beloved husband and he seems beaten, diminished. I adore him. I would kill for him.

"I have to make an appointment to take another drive test, if they let me."

I follow him back inside the DMV, he gets on a line, he gets an appointment for a month hence. He then has to go to the "Photo Room," where they take a picture to put on his temporary license. He looks like a dead man on the picture. His face is sunken and white, his eyes are blank.

We drive out of the DMV. I ask my husband if we can go to Chang's Garden for lunch. Some antidote to this poison is required. He just points the car toward home. We are on borrowed time here. He may have only days left to be my personal driver who takes me on our adventures, takes me to visit our distant children, takes me (rarely) to the beach so we can walk on Santa Monica Pier and let me play Skee Ball in the arcade.

Do I drive? I drove till a year ago when a big rig hit me on the freeway, spun me around into oncoming traffic whereupon two other trucks crashed into me. I had been on my way to the water-color painting class at the Cancer Support Center. Painting was

thought to be helpful and calming to those recovering from cancer treatment. My car was destroyed, I was banged up badly but
not killed. The shatter-proof glass of my Maxima shattered in little
jewel-like pieces all over my lap. As I sat there facing three lanes
of oncoming traffic, as I waited numbly for a Highway Patrol Officer to reach me, I gathered up some little glittering pieces of my
windshield and put them in my pocket for a souvenir. I knew was
never going to see this car again. So yes, I drive. I just don't go far,
not more than a mile or two and only when necessary. I drive to
my Depression Solutions group once a week. We talk about suicide
there, and other desperate matters.

We get home alive. In the garage, I step out of my shirt, my
pants, and my old sneakers and toss them in a pile. For good luck,
I peel off my underpants as well. I enter the house naked. I don't
explain the reasons for this to my husband.

Within days, the US mail brings an official letter from the DMV.
"The Department of Motor Vehicles has the responsibility of evalu-
ating drivers to ensure the safety of the motoring public. You must
have the enclosed medical forms completed by your doctor. If your
medical condition indicates an immediate risk to the public safety,
your driving privilege will be withdrawn and you will be notified
by mail." A six page medical evaluation form is enclosed, asking if
my husband has psychiatric disorders, types of dementia or cogni-
tive impairments, Alzheimer's, impulsive behavior, impaired language skills, depression secondary to dementia, impaired visual
spatial skills, and is he currently taking addictive drugs.

"Kafka had the same problems," my husband, the professor
that he is, says to me. But did Kafka have a wife like me who had
to call an HMO and arrange for all these forms to be filled out?

Life at home has changed considerably. My husband spends
hours at his computer playing "Free Cell," his jaw set. We don't talk.
We are under siege here and we are helpless. We are in a totalitar-
ian state.

In a few days, we go to the HMO to pick up the form completed by my husband's doctor. Under "Prognosis" he has merely written the word: "Fair."

"*Fair?*" I cry to my husband, as we examine the form in the waiting room. "Couldn't he have written *Good?*" My eye travels to the bottom of the page. Where it says "Date" the doctor has stamped his name and address, but he has not filled in a date. We go back to the desk, give the form to the receptionist and ask that the doctor date the document. Of course he is with a patient. Of course we have to wait another hour.

"Could we go to Chang's Garden for lunch?" I ask my husband. He doesn't seem to want hot and sour soup or fish in black bean sauce. He has hardly been eating these last days. His manhood is under threat. Sinister forces want to remove him from his vehicle, which in California is like being removed from your basic freedom to breathe.

My husband puts his arm around me. "Maybe tomorrow we can go to Chang's Garden."

There are lots of jokes about bad Chinese drivers. In Toronto, my friend Wing Ning tells me, a bumper sticker with the letter C on it adorns the cars of some Chinese drivers. I have read about an Asian woman who took the driving test 950 times before she passed!

At Chang's Garden I get fish filet with sweet and sour sauce, and my husband gets fish filet with black bean sauce. All around us sit Chinese diners—a sign, my husband says, that the food is good and authentic. What I feel, however, is that it's a sign that Chinese are taking over America, and that I am becoming the lonely outsider.

My husband has decided to take a refresher driving lesson and he makes an arrangement to do so. "Natividad" is going to be his date for this experience, and he goes off to the driving school in his car. He takes two lessons with her. Natividad gives him a letter stating that he is a good driver.

A legal letter arrives –my husband must appear at the Licensing Operations Division of the DMV to be interviewed under oath. A determination will then be made about his ability to take yet another driving test. We drive there, to an unfamiliar distant city, and when we get near to the required address, the GPS says, "Make a legal U-turn and then make a legal U-turn."

We have no idea what this means. Are we lost in some nightmare of DMV tricks? "Make a legal U-turn and then make a legal U-turn." The voice insists upon this. "Do it," I also insist. "Maybe she knows something we don't know."

I watch my husband make a legal U-turn and then as soon as he is able he makes another. But the GPS is right. After we make two legal U-turns, we find ourselves right in front of a huge building that says on it "STATE OF CALIFORNIA."

My husband's examiner, the letter says, will be Mr. Medrano. After a long wait, my husband is called in by Mr. Medrano. He is a short, dark-haired man, slightly balding.

"May I come in with him?" I ask and Mr. Medrano says, "Why, does he need your help?" Is he another Nazi? I see a sign on his office wall echoing one in the DMV stating that anyone threatening a state employee may be arrested and go to jail.

"This interview will be recorded, and we will now begin. Raise your right hand. Repeat after me: 'I swear that everything I say is the truth and nothing but the truth.'"

My husband swears. I don't see a bible. Maybe this is not the "so help me God" kind of oath. Mr. Medrano states that everything said here is for the record. He asks my husband his name, his address, his age. He stamps various things on his desk as evidence that must go into the record: the verified eye exam and the many-page medical form from my husband's doctor. There is also a note from Natividad of the driving school attesting that she has administered a two-day driving course.

Mr. Medrano asks my husband how bad his tremor is, does it get worse on different days, does it keep him from holding his hands on the steering wheel, does it interfere with his steering the car. My husband hesitates. He's thinking. I poke his thigh hard, out of sight of Mr. Medrano, to urge him to answer. Answer now!

Mr. Medrano announces that my husband will have to take a special drive-test with a specially trained instructor who is an expert on medical illnesses that impact driving safety. This examiner will have the ultimate decision about whether my husband will lose his driver's license.

We are dismissed. As we stand to leave, I venture one question.

"What if my husband fails that driving test—will he be allowed to take another?"

"Not if he makes a serious mistake that could put someone's life in danger."

This time, when we get into the car, I wonder, could my husband actually kill someone? Kill me? The GPS voice says: "Make a legal U-turn." But only one legal U-turn is required this time, and when my husband makes the turn, we are skillfully pointed in the direction of home.

When I can't sleep, I pick up "A Widow's Story," and allow myself to imagine my husband dead. But he isn't dead. How lucky I am! We could go on for years, we could live to a hundred. In bed, he still holds me tight.

The desperate widow is feeling abandoned, unprotected, stranded in her house that she once loved but now hates to enter. Still, friends surround her, feed her. She even gives a little dinner party in her own house and someone brings along a man she doesn't know, a professor at her college. This happens toward the end of her book where she is shown in a photo with her dead husband, and the words: "Of the widow's countless death-duties there is really just one that matters: on the first anniversary of her husband's death the widow should think *I kept myself alive.*"

On an impulse, I Google the writer's name. I discover that within a year of her husband's death, she eloped and married again. She married a good-looking Jewish guy from Brooklyn. Brooklyn, where I was born! I check her name under "Images" and there she is, the new bride, dancing with wild happiness at her wedding celebration given by friends, wearing a brilliant red satin coat, and kicking up her feet in joy.

How fair is that? How likely is that? If I were widowed, what are the chances of my finding a good-looking Jewish guy from Brooklyn? In fact, I am *married* to a good-looking Jewish guy from Brooklyn. Let me not go there. I never want the opportunity to find another. I have been in love with my husband for more than sixty years—may we live, as the saying goes, to 120.

My psychiatrist, who is a pretty young woman from the Philippines, wants me to add melatonin to the trazadone I take for sleep. She is dubious about my wanting to discontinue my antidepression drug which, as we have discussed before, has, in her words, "serious sexual side effects." Yes, this medicine kills all sexual desire in a tradeoff for a less depressed state of life. The puzzlement is this: how can one be less depressed if sex has flown from one's bed? She only allows me ten minutes, which is what the HMO permits for a checkup of one's psychotropic drugs and any adjustment that be required. "Do you have any stressful situations that may be coming up in your life?" the psychiatrist asks me, typing quickly on a keyboard in her lap as she speaks.

"Oh, not at all. Nothing stressful is coming my way."

In my Depression Solutions group, we do discuss the sex lives that are now our lot. One guy says that fifteen years ago he used to look like Brad Pitt and got laid twice a week. Now he gets all the affection that his mother never gave him from his dog. I love this group because even our therapist shares her troubles. She tells us about a theory of sharing pain, it's called "Tonglen." When we are suffering, we can do good in the world if we agree to take on the burdens of all others who are suffering and take the pain from them so they can be free of it for a time. We acknowledge this way that not only do we suffer, we all suffer. There's a breathing exercise that goes with this idea: take a deep breath, inhaling all the pain in the world, yours and others, and then blow it out, blowing away pain, freeing ourselves and others. Our therapist confides that she wants to have a husband one day, badly enough to take two weeks off for a little face lift and time to henna her hair. She, who is really young and gorgeous, says to our group that she envies me that I have been married so long. Is being envied a true satisfaction in life? I don't think so. Is my depression improving? I definitely am not going to take antidepressants any longer.

On the morning of the scheduled drive-test, I change my tactics. For breakfast, I make my husband French toast with fresh blueberries and pure maple syrup. I play a CD of Pachelbel as we eat and drink our coffee. I shower and apply coconut scented hair conditioner. I dress in my flowered chiffon dress with a lacy neckline and the wavy, uneven hem that moves delicately with every step. Finding a pair of gold and pearl earrings, I clip them on and slip my feet into my leather sandals. My husband, picking up the spirit of my mood, goes outside to polish the car. I help him by pointing at places he missed, little streaks on the windshield, a powdering of dust on the dashboard. We empty the back seat of all the bags now required to carry groceries out of Trader Joe's.

I pretend that we are not going to the DMV but on a road trip to Big Sur. My heart is light, my spirit excited, this will be a kind of honeymoon trip. I don't let my thoughts wander; I have blinkered them like a race horse's eyes to keep my focus.

I suggest to my husband that he wear the bright Hawaiian shirt I got him in the thrift shop. While he's in the bathroom, I use the attachment to his shaver to clip his sideburns neatly. He is so handsome, with his square jaw and his thrilling brown eyes. How lucky we have been all these years.

Nothing is going to stop us enjoying the rest of our lives, not some petty bureaucrat interfering in our plans. If he can't get his license, he'll just drive without one, he's never been stopped even once, ever, by a cop. We are going to overcome our troubles and transcend them.

While he gets dressed in his Hawaiian shirt and his brown dress pants, I go out in the yard and watch the hummingbirds dip into the sugar water in the hanging feeder. I practice "Tonglen" breathing, taking into myself all the suffering and troubles of the world, including ours, and then exhaling all the bitterness and pain upward to the exalted heavens.

Please, I say, *let these troubles be lifted from us.* To whom or what am I talking? It could be a hummingbird, what does it matter? It's out there or up there or in here.

"Okay, let's go," he says, "I'm ready."

"I'm ready, too."

This time I am not going to enter the DMV. Let my husband manage his necessities. When he parks, I wish him Godspeed and I take my little folding chair and my Kindle to a place in the shade and set myself up for the duration. I check the books I have recently downloaded: Being Mortal, Why Norma Jean Killed Marilyn Monroe, The Joys of Uncluttering Your House with Feng Shui, and You Are Always Safe with Me. The latter is a romance set in Turkey. I'll go for that.

I have a pretty sun-hat with me in case the glare gets too bright. I feel some sense of exultation which I do not question. There is a breeze coming over the tops of the cars waiting on line. Eventually I see my husband's car come around the corner. I just keep reading about the handsome Turkish captain sailing his little gulet through the inlets of the Turkish coastline and his attraction to the pretty woman who is one of the guests on the boat. By the time the other members of the cruise have gone on a shore excursion and the captain and the woman he loves are left alone on the deck of the boat, I am totally engrossed. There is a love scene, both delicate and sensual that takes place after the two of them kayak in the blue waters of the Mediterranean Sea. Though she may not be able to remain in Turkey with her lover, is it possible she might conceive his child? This is her desire and dream. The gulet rocks softly in the peaceful waters, the sunset sends a glaze of beauty that encloses them in a cocoon of love.

When my husband taps my arm and I look up, he nods at me. The examiner is walking ahead of him and holds the door of the DMV open for him and then he follows my husband inside.

Later that evening, my husband and I sit by the pool and appreciate the pandemonium of screaming parrots that cut across the streaks of sunset in the sky. My husband takes my hand—I feel no tremor in his. We are being mindful that summer is coming to an end, that the full moon will be overhead at midnight, that this winter El Nino may lessen the drought and our trees may not all die, but just a few. Later, when we go to bed, could it be? I have a shimmering sensation that the sexual side effects of my drug may be lifting.

A Life in Letters: A Decades-Long Correspondence with the Italian Writer Arturo Vivante

I N THE LATE 1950s, Arturo Vivante, an Italian doctor living in Rome, began publishing short stories in the *New Yorker*. I was a young writer at the time, studying with Andrew Lytle at the University of Florida. Vivante's stories, written in English, seemed so alive and true. They created in me an energy that sent me back to my dorm room to write late into the night.

By the time I finished a year of graduate school, I had sold a story to *Mademoiselle,* and in 1962, I took up residence with my husband, Joe, and new baby daughter at Stanford, where I had been selected to be a Wallace Stegner Fiction Fellow. The first two stories I wrote in Stegner's workshop were brazenly lifted from real life. "A Daughter of My Own" depicted the time when my mother came to "help out" with our baby and ended up intruding almost violently into the life of our family. "We Know That Your Hearts Are Heavy" was about the funeral of my father's brother, where, when the coffin was brought into the synagogue, I heard for the first time my father sobbing, almost choking, with grief. To my astonishment, I sold both stories, the first to *Redbook*, the second to the *New Yorker*. What luck!

I knew I had revealed too many secrets, but I took courage from what Vivante dared to do. His story "The Wide Sleeping Bag," published in the *New Yorker* in 1958, begins:

Sometimes I wish things so intensely they happen. But the circumstances through which they come about, the ways chosen to let me have what I want, are invariably quite different from those I had in mind. It's as if Fate cared only about the end, not the means . . .

The narrator takes a summer job with the Forest Service, working with a man who goes around the woods of the Canadian North with his wife, looking for the budworms that destroy the trees.

I was eighteen, given to wild dreams, very apt to fall in love at first sight . . .

My boss's wife was pretty . . . Sometimes she washed her hair in the lake, and then for a long time she combed it in the sun . . . Sometimes at night I used to hear them laughing together. The laughing would fade into whispers, the whispers fade into silence . . .

I thought I loved her. I thought I loved her far more than he did.

During a budworm expedition, the woman falls seriously ill. Her husband must take a boat across the lake to find a doctor, leaving the young man in charge. During the night, the boss's wife is stricken with a terrible chill. She thinks she is going to die and invites the young man into her sleeping bag. Intending only to keep her warm, he removes his shoes and slips in beside her.

"Hug me tight," she said . . .

"Tighter."

I hugged her as tight as I could. For a while she continued shivering; then she stopped . . . I sensed that the heat of my body had done something to her . . .

"Ah, I feel better now," she said.

"I am glad, I am glad."

"You are very warm."

"Yes," I said.

I was sure that Vivante himself had experienced something similar, creeping into that wide sleeping bag and later bravely and with inspiration turning reality into art.

After leaving Stanford, we settled in Southern California, where Joe took a job as a professor of history, and I stayed home caring for our baby, having a second and then a third daughter, all within five years. My little girls played at my feet as I wrote on my typewriter in our living room.

Around the time my first book of stories appeared, I discovered a new collection of Vivante's: *The French Girls of Killini*. I bought it and noticed it was dedicated to Vivante's editor at the *New Yorker*, Rachel MacKenzie, who had been my editor there, too.

I wrote him a letter in care of his publisher:

Dear Mr. Vivante—

It seems [from your stories] as though simple things cheer you, and though I hope you are not in need of cheering now that your book is being opened all over the country, I want to say it is a lovely book, and a lovely soul shines through to light every page.

*I write in a spirit of both emotional and professional admiration . . . and, as a number of people felt obliged to apologize when they wrote me about my own collection of stories [*Stop Here, My Friend*], "I am not given to writing fan letters."*

But I am not moved by too much modern fiction, either, and I had to make some outward response.

Best,
Merrill Joan Gerber

His reply came a month later from his family villa in Siena:

Dear Merrill Joan Gerber,

I received your letter today. It is a rare and beautiful letter. Thank you more than I can say. One responsive reader makes writing a book worthwhile. On such consonance of feelings my mind thrives.

I am so glad you told me about your work. I am eager to read your stories, and I am ordering your collection of them. Thank you again.

All my very best wishes,
Arturo Vivante

Two months later, I received another letter, not from Italy but from America, where he had moved in 1958. Selling stories, one after the other, to the *New Yorker,* he was earning more as a writer than as a doctor. In 1957, he had met a young American woman, Nancy Bradish, who had come into his practice with a minor ailment, and married her a year later. They were now living with their children in Wellfleet, Massachusetts.

Dear Merrill Joan Gerber,

I have now received and read Stop Here, My Friend. *I was greatly impressed by the power of your writing. I don't know how I missed the two [stories] that appeared in the* New Yorker. *I especially liked "The Cost Depends on What You Reckon It In." What a fine story! The word story seems hardly enough for it, too little for it—it is life unfolding. It is so genuine and so forceful and you are so spirited—in each one of your stories. I was struck also by your picture on the book jacket. It has an Athena-like quality.*

All my very, very best wishes to you,
Yours cordially,
Arturo Vivante

Immediately, I went to examine my picture on the book jacket. There was my regular face, which I was so used to seeing—in what way did it have an "Athena-like quality"? I began to see myself in a different light. I felt a rush of such gratitude! Heartfelt praise from Arturo Vivante. I had somehow stepped into the best moment of my life.

However, Fate had a hand in changing my situation: at age 55, my father became ill with leukemia, and within three months he was dead. I continued to relive his all-consuming suffering, moment by moment. My mother was stricken and nearly helpless in her grief, and I found myself unable to write. Any diversion felt somehow like a betrayal of his anguish. For a year I struggled, unable to play with my children, or even take any pictures of them.

Later, I would encounter Vivante's story "The Bell," which dealt with a son coming to terms with his father's illness—"a slow and endless decline till the son begins wishing the end would arrive":

"What is death like, I wonder," he asked his father one such time . . .
"It is a dim gray ward in which your senses fade little by little."
And his son thought, This is the true picture. And, He's perfectly
right not to want to die. He has seen death, knows it from close by,
has seen its gorge . . . And the son thought of the orange eye of a cat
gone opaque and dull . . . From that time on, he didn't increase the
dosage [of the sleeping drops], not even by one drop, and though be-
fore he had wished—hoped—for his father's death, he didn't now.

My father had also seen death up close. Mustard gas was a desperate, experimental treatment then for leukemia. On the day he died, he said to my mother, my sister, and me: "There are going to be a lot of people in this room tomorrow night. There are going to be a lot of chairs in here. Listen! Do you hear the knocking at the secret door? If you'll be quiet for a minute, you'll hear it."

None of us heard the knocking.

Eventually, I found the energy to begin writing a book about my father's death. I wrote it in a frenzy of anguish and relief. By pouring into *An Antique Man* all I could remember about my father's illness, I was secure in knowing I had honored his agonies and ours. Once the experience was safely between the covers of a book, I began to breathe freely again. I could hold my children and laugh with them. I could embrace my husband.

On June 23, 1967, Arturo scrawled this note to me in pencil from New York City:

Dear Merrill,

We are just about to sail for Italy, hence this hurried note. I did want to tell you, though, that I saw Rachel [MacKenzie at the New Yorker] yes-

terday. She is well, and spoke of you and of your book with admiration.
She said it was very moving; that she wept throughout, and that she had
also shown it to [William] Shawn. She means to write to you.

I did hear from Rachel MacKenzie—she told me that they had
tried to find an excerpt from my manuscript that would stand
alone in the magazine, but alas, they had not found a section that
would work for them.

Within a couple of weeks, she wrote to me again. Her boss,
William Shawn, could not get the book out of his mind, and would I
please send the manuscript back to them. I did so at once, and lived
in a state of almost unbearable tension, waiting for a reply. When
the second rejection came, it was far worse than the first—they had
concluded that a section of at least 100 pages was needed to stand
alone, and that was too long for the magazine.

Vivante's stories continued to be a guide for me as, in his fiction, he worked his way through painful, and sometimes joyful, life
experiences. "The Binoculars" is about a man whose mother has
died before he can fulfill a promise to her.

"How I'd like to go to the Abruzzi to buy dishes!" his mother
often said . . . "Just you and I in your little car—with room for only
the dishes in the back . . . Shall we go? Shall we go?" . . . But they
hadn't got around to going.

Then she had fallen ill . . .

It was four months now since she had died.

Some years before her death, the son in the story had stopped
in an Abruzzi mountain village where he found a little ceramics
shop that sold dishes—"each cup, vase, plate, and saucer had a
painting—a landscape with trees, a brook, a little house, and mountains in the background." He had brought several dishes home to
his mother. She had adored them, and begged to go with him so
they could buy more. "Now it was too late to take her. Still, he felt
he should make the trip—felt it almost as a duty."

He travels to another remote village. He has with him a pair of binoculars that he uses on the trip to admire the mountains, the details of the little houses high in the hills, the colors of the wash hanging out to dry. When he stops at a ceramics shop, he buys nearly everything in sight, soup plates, cups, saucers, a vase . . . When he gets back to his car with his bounty of dishes, he discovers that his binoculars are gone. Some villagers tell him that an "odd" boy had no doubt taken them, a boy who had stolen before. The police are called, the binoculars are recovered, the boy is taken to the town hall. All seems to have gone wrong with this trip. The story concludes:

A few days later, at the table, waiting for food to be passed round, he stared into his empty plate. . . . What he saw was not the open sky, the little silver cloud . . . the flowers but a barred window.

"Aren't these plates lovely!" a guest said to him . . .

"Yes," he said. "Yes. Lovely."

He thought, the binoculars stolen, the boy in jail, and this woman here instead of my mother—they are all in keeping with each other.

Vivante, pictured here with his son Benjamin in 1968, noted the "Athena-like quality" of Gerber's dust-jacket photo. (left: Val Cheney; center: Bernard Gotfryd; right, at Solaia, Siena, c. 1950)

In 1970, my husband and I took a trip to Italy. I had written to Arturo that we were coming, and he had sent me his phone number, saying I must be certain to call him. I dialed Siena from our hotel room in Florence. A woman answered the phone, saying, *"Pronto!"* She called Arturo's name. There was a long pause, and then a tired, almost exhausted voice answered, saying, "Yes?" I told him who I was and asked if we might stop in to visit him at his home for a little while. "Yes, of course, yes, come, please, do."

I asked what might be a good time, and he said, "We have lunch at 1:30, please come, it won't be any trouble. Let me give you directions to the villa." He instructed me in a distracted, wavery voice as I took it all down on hotel stationery.

"I'm looking forward to meeting you," I said. "I can't tell you how much!"

"Yes, I'm looking forward as well." There was a pause, and then he said, "Who did you say it was? I didn't quite get your name."

"Oh my God," I said to Joe after I'd hung up. "He doesn't even know who I am!"

Villa Solaia was a pale-yellow house at the top of a long hill. I was struck by the silence around us, not a bird calling, not a breeze stirring, just intense yellow heat, and silence. Joe and I crunched on pebbles as we approached the front door. Arturo was waiting inside the dim doorway, much heavier and older than his book jacket had pictured him. "Hello, welcome to the villa," he said, and shook my hand and then Joe's. Did he now know who I was? I thought I might say how peaceful it must be to live in the country, how conducive to work, how inspiring, but Arturo was shuffling his way down the dim hallway, murmuring, "Something to drink." He returned with two glasses of wine. I took a sip, but it was bitter, and I set the glass down on a wooden table. There was the tinny sound of a cowbell, and Arturo said, "That will be lunch."

We followed him through a dim, oddly cool hallway to a room where a huge dining table was set with many white plates. So this was the famous villa I had read about in his stories, the one where Americans and other tourists in Tuscany came to stay. Their patronage helped to support the upkeep of the big house and all its servants. Arturo's wife came toward us introducing herself—a pretty woman with long brown hair laced with gray, and wearing a plain loose dress and beach slippers. "Please, you sit here, next to Arturo," she said, and pulled out a chair for me at the table. She led my husband to the other side of the table, where she offered him a seat next to her. Around her were her three children, two little girls, and a curly-haired younger boy. Others came to the table, various travelers talking about pasta machines and luggage allowances and leather goods in Siena.

A man looking much like Arturo, who must have been his brother, was sitting farther down the table, smoking a pipe, appearing indifferent to the activity around us. I finally said to Arturo, "Your writing has meant a great deal to me," but I saw at once he did not want to hear this, so I said quickly, "Do you often have guests here?"

"Very often," he said. "Nearly always."

"Does it interfere with your work, having so many people around all the time?"

"Sometimes they give me an idea." Then he added, "They used to."

An elderly servant woman came in wheeling a wagon holding an enormous steaming bowl of pasta and served each of the diners. Arturo passed a full bowl to me and began eating, so I ate silently beside him. After a time, I ventured another question: "Do you have a favorite among your stories?"

"I am tired of my own work. I am tired of thinking about what I did. I'm not doing anything now."

"Do you know which story is my favorite?" I persisted. "The one in which the man goes to the Abruzzi to buy dishes for his mother, and then his binoculars are stolen."

Suddenly, Arturo leaned back in his chair and stretched his arm behind him to open a cupboard against the wall. He pointed to the lower shelf, and there I saw the piles of hand-painted dishes that he must have bought for his mother.

I nearly gasped. "Oh!" I said. "I've always felt your stories ring with true life."

"As do yours," he said, and briefly put his hand over mine on the table. "As do yours." And with relief I knew he knew who was sitting beside him.

After lunch, he walked my husband and me to the door. I said, "We are planning to reach Rome tonight, so we must leave now. But thank you so much for having us here to visit you. I will be looking for more of your stories."

"At the moment," he said, looking past me toward the hills, "there is nothing much to watch for."

Inspiration must have returned, because I count 25 stories of Vivante's from 1970 to 1981 that I clipped and saved from *New Yorker* magazines. During those years, when he was living mainly in Massachusetts and teaching at different colleges, we exchanged many letters and sent each other books we'd written.

In 1993, I asked if he might write a reference letter for me to the Guggenheim selection committee. "I am hardly the right person to ask," he responded, "since of all the many writers I've recommended for it not one has received it—I'm just not influential enough, and little known. Also, in my old age, I've become very forgetful and weary."

I replied:

> Don't worry about writing a Guggenheim reference letter. I have applied more than a dozen times and my turn-down letter always arrives on my birthday. . . . It is devastating at times to be a writer. Here is a letter of rejection I just got from an editor about my 800-page, three generation family novel, The Victory Gardens of Brooklyn . . . *"Page by page this is far superior to most of the coming-to-America novels that I've*

published. The story has a leisurely observant quality that's at odds with the requirements of the genre: Bottom line—it's good but needs a great schlocky melodramatic plot!" There are days I feel that being a writer is no more than begging and being bludgeoned.

His reply:

Your feelings are familiar. I can certainly identify with them. . . . To be a great success, such as Picasso was, you need to be a mirror of the times, which may not be all that desirable, the times being what they are. And then success isn't the utmost of values; it could be viewed as an enviable state, and the wish to be successful as a wish to be envied. It also has to do with ambition, pride, power, and little to do with what really matters: inspiration, insight, wisdom. At best, it is satisfaction of recognition and testimony of one's value, but not as sweet as honey, more like beet root. And the best seller lists are so appalling. Your writing is so live and tuneful!

Arturo and I continued to write frequently, and sometimes he sent me postcards filled with his tiny, wavering handwriting. When he was 82, and we had corresponded with each other for 40 years, I confessed to him that I had written a story about our visit to Villa Solaia and had sent it, in the 1970s, to Rachel MacKenzie. She told me they "couldn't touch it," since so many writers had visited Villa Solaia and had written stories about it over the years. Arturo begged to see my story. I found a yellowed, tattered carbon copy, which I sent to him. On August 8, 2005, he wrote:

Thank you so much for sending your story, "The Villa." It is so very accurate in every detail, and you capture the atmosphere of the house admirably. I often regret having agreed to its sale. Your story, however, led me to think that the villa flourished in the 1950's and 1960's, and that, even if we had kept it, it would have been hard put to flourish again, like people, perhaps. Some of the lines brought a smile, or rather a laugh, to my face, e.g., "both brothers wore a certain detached, patient air about them—not sad, not depressed so much as resigned and willing to en-dure." The lines show your skill in characterization that I have admired again and again, I recognize most people, and especially myself in the story!

After Arturo's wife, Nancy, died in 2002, his sense of gloom increased. That he had sold more than 70 stories to the *New Yorker* over his lifetime, an incredible achievement, seemed not to sustain him. He felt himself to be "little known and uninfluential."

"I am not terribly well," he wrote, "have a hard time walking any distance and drive almost everywhere, and often I find it hard to write even a letter."

Yet in 2004, the University of Notre Dame Press published a book of his short stories, *Solitude*. He sent me a copy, and being so familiar with many of the stories, I thought I should review it. My review appeared in the *Los Angeles Times* on July 24, 2005. "Unlike Chekhov," I wrote, who called medicine his lawful wife and literature his mistress, Arturo Vivante gave up medicine entirely when, as a young doctor in Rome, he began to sell his stories to the *New Yorker* and decided writing was his true calling. Both professions require attention to the dimensions of suffering and pain, although Vivante seems to have been drawn more to the pain of the psyche than to the pain of the body.

I noted that Vivante "muses on the essential loneliness of our human existence and our yearning for connection." And I wrote about how love "is a primary force in these stories, although not necessarily the love of a man and his wife."

Arturo responded to my review:

What a delight to receive your letter with your splendid review of Soli-tude. . . . Your review is the best I've ever had and it came at a time when I couldn't have needed more encouraging to start writing again. . . . I think readers will be drawn to buy the book since the review is very inviting and the quotations very apt.

His energy seemed to rise. Within weeks, he told me that he had revised a novel he had written 10 years before. Then, some weeks later:

Merrill, here is my novel Truelove Knot. *Thank you for being willing to read it. If it is a burden or you don't have time, send it back, I enclose an envelope. When I wrote the novel I thought it was my best work but now I just don't know. They often say that writers aren't the best judges of their work. I certainly value your opinion and would be extremely interested to hear what you think of it.*

I made some suggestions for changes, which he incorporated into the text. Shortly thereafter he wrote:

Notre Dame Press sent me the contract and I signed it on the theory that an egg today is better than a chicken tomorrow. 'Meglio un uovo oggi che una gallina domani.'

Despite his rise in spirits, he found himself growing weaker:

It would be lovely to meet you and your husband when you visit your daughter in Washington this winter, but oh dear I am getting so old and a long trip worries me. I have terrible dreams of getting lost in strange cities. I should go to Italy one last time to look after my little apartment in Bomarzo which I bought after my family sold Villa Solaia in Siena. My children seem to have little time or inclination to go there for any length of time but they don't want to sell it. I bought a computer, hearing aids, and I use a cane for any distance outdoors.

After getting the computer, Arturo seemed triumphant in his ability to use email, and his letters came to me with a new look and a new speed. Then another piece of good news came his way. The Academy of Arts and Letters in New York was to give him the Katherine Anne Porter Prize, with an award of $20,000. "You are the only writer I am corresponding with now," he wrote. "Inspiration, I expect, will visit you unannounced and you will soon be writing a new story."

And then:

At the awards ceremony in New York I was approached by an agent, but the University of Notre Dame Press had already accepted the novel. . . . [T]he ceremony went well though the trip was rather tiring as was my recent journey to Italy. It was pleasant to walk around the old streets of Rome and to be at my village in Bomarzo where I spent most of my time. The atmosphere was very festive with a concert right in my little piazza which I viewed from my balcony. At one point a young man stood up and played a clarinet solo very melodiously.

In August 2006, there was another surprise:

I sent Solitude *to a girl I wrote about long ago in the* New Yorker, *May 1982, who is my daughter. Her mother came to Villa Solaia in 1967 with her husband. . . . He was away for two weeks. I went for a walk in the woods with his wife and a year later she called me to come and see her in Florence. I went and she told me that I was the father of a little girl. I saw her and held her in my arms. . . . When the girl was ten, her mother died of a heart attack and her father died, too. . . . For years I didn't have the heart to reach her. But I finally sent her my book with a note saying I was a friend of her mother. She immediately phoned me. She is a brunette and suspected that her father wasn't her father. A week ago she flew here and we had a very happy reunion.*

Arturo told me he felt ill and weak, that everything he was doing now was a move to "concluding"—his last visit to Bomarzo, meeting his daughter again, and then her meeting his children at his home in Wellfleet—"a jolly time we had, eleven around the table." And his letters came less often.

I wrote to him about having an abnormal EKG and being rushed to a hospital to have an angiogram. "No one could find either vein or artery," I wrote, "and other doctors had to be called in—by the end of it my leg was deeply mashed up. Though they didn't find blocked arteries they did find a thickened heart muscle, so we are in deep waters here, you and I."

His reply, the last letter he sent me, on December 23, 2007, moved me almost to tears:

Dear Merrill, your description of the tests and exams that you endured strikes a sensitive and familiar note. Your dear heart! Your limbs that should not know needles and electrodes but rather kisses and caresses.

Yet I also had to smile, knowing that Arturo had charmed women all his life. I recalled the wife's words in the story "Company": "you and all your girlfriends . . ."

In that same letter, he also told me he had been diagnosed with cancer:

There are no particular treatments for me except symptomatic ones. I am not particularly calm but the pain is very slight and temporary and is taken care of by the analgesics.

Thank you for your second email about [my mention in] the New Yorker. Vanity is present even when one is ill and I appreciate your telling me about it. I had not seen it, though. [My daughter] Lydia will get one for me tomorrow.

Love, Arturo

Arturo died on April 1, 2008. His daughters and son dispersed his ashes to the ocean that he loved, on the night of a full moon in Wellfleet.

Two days after I finished writing this essay, I stopped at a little thrift shop in my town. A man had come in to donate a pile of dishes, which he left on the counter. The dishes were delicately painted with sprays of tulips, roses, and poppies all rising from a starburst of lacy green leaves. I turned one over. It was signed with the artist's name and the town in Italy in which it was painted. In a state of astonishment, I bought all the dishes for one dollar each and took them home, where I put them with a sense of reverence in my dining room cabinet.

The Found Desk

RIDAY NIGHT, the night before my husband's birthday, we were taking our usual walk around the block at almost nightfall. Suddenly, I saw in the street before us a small antique desk, put out for the taking. I was overcome with a desire for it; I had a flashlight with me and shone it upon the desk. I saw that it was covered in layers of dust. With my handkerchief I cleaned a small area and saw a circle of gleaming dark walnut emerge. The desk had two cubbyholes and two little drawers inlaid with mother-of-pearl. Its legs were delicately carved. The whole creation was quite small, but beautiful. I opened the drawers . . . in one of them were some tiny cracked balloons, a small bottle of Chanel No. 5 and in the other drawer was a key and a coin. I tried to pick up the coin, a dime, but it seemed glued to the bottom of the drawer.

"I want this desk," I told my husband. "Would you pick up one side so we can see if it's not too heavy for us to put in the back of the car?"

He stepped far back from the desk. "No," he said.

"But I want it," I said. "It's perfect. It's beautiful. It's a treasure."

He stepped even further back from the thing as if it were a dead animal. He was standing in the middle of the street. If a car had come along, it could have killed him.

"Oh please," I said. "Let's not get into one of these discussions, I want it, let's just go home and get the car. Or you go home and get the car and I'll stand here and guard the desk. Otherwise someone might grab it."

I waited for discussion, but none came. He was perfectly silent. I shone the flashlight sideways at his face to see what I knew was there: utter disgust with me. I had seen that look before, once when we were walking on a street in Florence and I'd seen a pile of magazines put out at the curb and I picked up a few to take back to our apartment so I could read them. He'd been humiliated then, too— because three Italian ladies had seen me pick them up and were scowling at me.

He simply couldn't deal with the truth that I, his wife, was a garbage collector.

"But think of the *new* things we're getting," I said, with concession in my voice. "That you *insisted* on, the couch and chair coming back from the upholsterer tomorrow. The new look you wanted after so many years. I loved that couch—how our girls played on it when they were little! I could feel their shapes in the cushions . . . but I said okay. Didn't I I let them carry half my life into that truck last week because you wanted it? So why not let me have this desk? It will be new to us. Once I clean it up, it could fit against that wall . . ."

My husband began walking away, walking home without me.

I shot a glance of longing at the desk. I took from its drawers the tiny balloons, the perfume. I had already put the key into my pocket. With my cell phone, I tried to take a picture of the desk in the dark. Even if I aimed the flashlight at it, the camera would capture nothing but a blur. My heart was skipping beats. I began to walk toward home. I couldn't, by myself, carry the desk on my back. He had refused me. He looked ugly, like a gorilla with flat feet, stomping home, up ahead.

It was now dark on the street. In the many uncurtained windows of the houses around us, I could see enormous televisions blasting their images into living rooms and family rooms. All of us in the world were getting the same news, the same gossip, the same visions of kidnapped children and serial killers and crashed planes and sports heroes. The same faces visited us night after night, and talked to us and to all our neighbors and all our countrymen. Our eyes were blasted with suicide bombers and pirate ships and war dead and corrupt politicians and workplace mass murders, and rap stars and ball games. I was so tired of the world and everything in it. God, how old I felt. My husband and I had been married such an incredibly long time.

What if I'd married a man who loved old furniture, who thrilled at buying derelict antiques at flea markets and carrying them home like trophies, who refinished them and proudly displayed them? What if I'd married a man, now that I was imagining, who loved animals, went walking in the woods every morning with two big hunting dogs (and his rifle?) Or a man who loved to garden, who grew enormous pumpkins and entered them in contests? Or a fellow who bonded with his buddies—the kind of guy who had lots of friends and entertained them at barbecues in the yard with tall stories, jokes, and cases of beer?

The husband I'd married didn't even watch football. He never lit a barbecue. He had been in his youth the most beautiful and delicious of all young men; his beauty had made me cry. And how he said he loved me, then, and sometimes now. His longing and desire for me shone in the way he looked at me, told me his feelings had not changed one bit. Still, at our last anniversary I *counted* that we had slept together more than 18,000 thousand nights. I tried to imagine any one of them, but not one came to mind. If only I could re-live just one of them—right now. Tonight. Did he ever think such thoughts? Had I ever asked him? In his retirement, he played Bach partitas for entertainment. He studied languages for fun. Sometimes I'd come into his office to tell him lunch was ready and he'd be playing Scrabble on his computer. We no longer played Scrabble together, with wooden tiles at the kitchen table as we used to do. Now we each played separately, on our own computers. It was faster that way, and private. Like pornography. No pausing for the needs of the other.

I lost sight of him ahead of me in the street. I kept the flashlight turned off, placing him in danger. There were no streetlights in our neighborhood. On moonless nights, it was dark as a tomb on these streets. What if he were hit by a car? I'd have to bury him.

A block from our house was The Pioneer Cemetery—set in a woodsy corner of the city, with headstones dating back to the Civil War. Angels sat on many of them. Marble benches were placed overlooking family gravesites and often, as we walked through the grassy pathways, we saw presents left for the dead, little white-faced china dolls, American flags, a toy piano. Now and then we saw a burial taking place . . . family members standing in the grass. One day we saw a Scottish bagpipe player blowing mournful tunes over the graves.

Recently, almost as often as my husband and I had argued about re-upholstering the couch, we had talked about where we should deposit our dead bodies. I thought I had already solved this problem after my mother died. By then, my father had been dead thirty-two years. I decided to follow ads in the obituary section of the newspaper where one day I found a pair of used graves for sale in the Jewish cemetery where my parents were buried. I managed to buy them from a man who was moving back to New York and planned to die there with his wife. I could see that these particular grave sites were a steal—not two steps from the curving road near the cemetery entrance but also under two canopied shade trees. These were prime sites. Dead Jews were overrunning the cemetery, which had begun expanding up into the hills, then into even higher and rockier hills. At present the earthmovers were digging grave sites that were almost inaccessible. And the cemetery was selling them for more than twice what we had paid.

Now that we were as old as we had become, I had recently inquired about the cost of burial there. The cemetery sent me the facts: to own the gravesites was barely the beginning. I had a list of what was required for us to be deposited in consecrated Jewish ground: "Basic services, $1,350." "Transfer of remains, $375." (Wasn't that a basic service?) "Standard preparation: $450." (What was that?) "Embalming: $450"—we weren't interested in embalming.) "Use of equipment: $625." "Use of funeral coach: $100." "Outer burial vault (grave liner): $550." "Cemetery charges—Open/Close: $800." There were the recommended optionals: Burial shroud, $105, Ziegler container, $475 (if necessary for plane transport to the grave), Ritual cleaning $200, Sh'mira, minimum for 12 hours $180. Newspaper notice, $100, Limousine, $700+, Flowers, $400+. Rabbi Honorarium, $500 +, and Memorial tablet $2000+.

All these thousands, just for dying?

"Fuck it," I said, as I followed my husband home. "Fuck dying." My language had become rougher in the last few years. I wasn't the girl he had married. *Commit me*, I sent the message to the back of his head. *Or divorce me.*

Friends of mine were dying already. Constance died from breast cancer that had turned her breast black ("A skin disorder," is what she told me she had. "I don't go to doctors," she said. "I hate death.") She was cremated and her grandson dropped her ashes (from a little plastic sand pail) into the ash garden of The Pioneer Cemetery. How clean and easy it seemed to me—whereas now and then I dreamed of my mother who was buried in the Jewish cemetery in her red bathrobe with little boats on it; in my dreams I wondered how much of the cloth was left hanging on her bones. And her skull, how did it look? All her teeth had been pulled when she was thirty, to treat her migraines. Her skull could never be identified by dental records now if she had to be exhumed. My mother's and father's bones, lying under the dirt—they rose up in my dreams.

After my friend died of breast cancer, we often had dinner with her husband at a neighborhood Mexican restaurant. He was a tall, thin, good-looking scientist who studied stars. His daughter and her family lived in Montana. Learning to live alone (with just his dog), he began to take cruises with investment-themed seminars on them. He boarded the dog when he was away. On Father's Day his daughter phoned to say she couldn't reach her father—did we know where he was? Was he on a cruise?

I said we'd had dinner with him a week ago—but hadn't heard from him since. I told her to check with his next-door neighbor. The neighbor called the police. My friend's husband was found dead—collapsed in his nightshirt on the floor next to his bed. Dead for a week, they said. His German shepherd had also perished after drinking all the water in the toilet bowls and shredding the bag of dog food in the laundry room.

Husband and dog were cremated, too—and their ashes were poured by the same grandson, now two years older, and grown strong in Montana, into the same ash garden where his grandmother was dropped. The ash garden could hold thousands of dead people—ashes were ephemeral, an infinity of them could fit in a little garden. A plaque for each of our friends was installed on the wall of the ash garden. Constance's plaque read, "Home Free," and her husband's read, "From the Prairies to the Stars."

The Pioneer Cemetery featured many graves with crosses on them. I thought we should buy plots for ourselves there. They were cheap. The place was close to home. But exactly how Jewish were we? Were we obligated to support the Jewish community in death when we had not bothered doing much about it in life? And what made Jewish ground sacred? The plots we already owned were in a cemetery right next to Forest Lawn, which featured numerous churches for weddings as well as funerals, a kissing bench for newly married couples, a reproduction of Michelangelo's "Moses" and one of The Last Supper reconstituted in stained glass. On the grounds were acres of mausoleums where movie stars and others who feared earth-burial were hoisted into vaults high above the ordinary ground. But these two cemeteries, these two burials parks, side by side, were made of the same dirt from the same hills. Did God look down and distinguish between Jewish dirt and Christian dirt? I was missing the point, of course, but all rules and religions emerging from the social order seemed ridiculous to me, such as the rule about not picking up items discarded into the gutter. My husband's mother had always bought new furniture. My father, an antique dealer, had never bought anything new. All our furniture had been second-hand. Everything in his store had a history, a former use, a value that had been suddenly interrupted by some terrible event, the dissolution of a home or a marriage, an incurable illness, the end of a life.

We were approaching our house. Our pool wall was in sight at the corner of the street. Two years ago, a woman moved in opposite our house and when I introduced myself in the manner of a Welcome Wagon greeter: ("Hi, you must be our new neighbor . . . " and extended my hand), the woman said to me, "I have to stare at this eyesore of your pool wall from my living room window every day." I took back my hand. I glanced at my pool wall made of concrete blocks that were painted a pleasant pink color. "Eyesore?" I asked.

"Look, I'm a decorator," she said. "I charge $125 an hour for advice, but for you, I'd give it free, and explain how you could transform that pool wall into something decent for me to look at."

"Maybe some other time," I said, and went back into the house. Did I even want to be buried in this California neighborhood after all? So many of my neighbors seemed lacking in human decency and ordinary friendliness. Where was my real home? Brooklyn, where I was born? Maybe I should be buried there. In the cemetery where my grandmother was buried, with Hebrew letters on her leaning tombstone. Where death looked like death.

My husband had now entered the front door of our house but didn't glance behind him or wait for me. He went in without me and left the door open for flies to come in.

How could you! I thought. *I wanted that desk. How dare you think you can give me permission or not? How dare you try to control me? What about a room of my own? Maybe I need a house of my own!*

And what now? It was the eve of his birthday. Celebrations were imminent. Tomorrow the new couch and chair, empty of history and meaning, were arriving. Two of our daughters were coming for lunch. And after *this*, I was supposed to cook my husband a celebratory meal?

When I got in the door, my husband was not in sight. I presumed he had gone down the hall and was already playing Scrabble on his computer. I had somehow to fill the hours until bedtime. In trying to get the house organized for the delivery of the couch and chair, I had been cleaning up the debris of forty years of living in one place. On the dining table was a box of my ancient papers and letters. A notebook from my piano lesson days was among them with a program featuring my piano teacher on the inside cover: "Gwendlyn Haber, Pianiste, Carnegie Music Hall, June 12, 1947. She'd be dead now, probably, but there on the first page of the notebook in her hand-writing was: "This is F, this is C, In between lies D and E." And then dozens of pages, years worth of pages of my dreaded piano lesson assignments. My husband would have loved it if I'd played duets with him over the years. But I never wanted to. I'd disappointed him. I didn't want him standing over me telling me how to play and practice.

Also, there in the box was a sheet of onion skin paper:

THOUGHTS ON MY FIRST NIGHT AWAY FROM HOME AT COLLEGE: September 22, 1955. "I can see a girl through the window, crying. I want to cry, too . . . no one cares about me here, it is so lonely, what do all these silly girls mean to me, all they talk about is boys, boys, boys, how could I begin to tell them the things dearest to my heart, how much I love my boyfriend, how I miss him. Why are we apart in different colleges? How can I live without him? I am in love and I cry till I could die."

Just the scribbling of a lovesick young girl. And what of the beloved boyfriend—wasn't he the very same human being who had just walked in the front door without me? What else was in the box? Oh yes, a folder of letters written by my mother-in-law to my husband when he was in college. I knew these letters by heart but had not seen them in many years. How the woman had hated my guts! But why? Till I met her, everyone had loved me. I was a good girl, I was a good student. I was smart and polite. No one had any reason to hate me till she came along.

His mother wrote: "I hope you will realize the seriousness of our little heart-to-heart talk (monologue) and extricate yourself at once from any 'steady' or even any suggestion of 'steady' alliance. It is all too easy to get involved and tied up at an early age, only to be sorry when it is too late. You haven't even begun to live, and you have too much to learn and to do and to see and too many people to meet, to get tied up at the ridiculous age of eighteen. This is the time to realize all this, and call a halt to this business NOW! I could say much more on this subject, but you know how I feel and perhaps you have given this some more thought and have realized that YOU ARE IN A NET—SO GET OUT NOW! If you were home this summer, would you spend all your free time with HER, and also quite a bit of money, tying yourself down to a steady girl, who, let us be frank, is not the best you could do. You picked the first thing that came along—not beautiful, not from a well-off family, a flat-chested girl who is always hanging on to your hand as if she's afraid you will drop her and run off."

Now, oddly, I was thinking how she may have been right—no mother would want her son to get hung up with a flat-chested, not beautiful and not rich girl, especially at the age of eighteen. How clearly I could see her point. What if her son had taken her advice and dropped my hand? Dropped me by the wayside, and then I too would have moved on and begun to meet new people. By now I would surely have a different husband living with me in some other house, (possibly a richer husband though not likely handsomer, but definitely one who loved his wife so much he would single-handedly have wanted to carry that found desk back to the house for her. Right now he'd be admiring her sharp eye for treasures, he'd be kissing her entire body as a reward for her brilliance in finding a treasure on the curbside, in plain view).

I began thinking again about my own dying, this most inconvenient and unpleasant interruption certain to arrive, inevitable and non-negotiable. Why be buried at all—but instead why not be cremated and sent out on the wind into the blessed essence of nature? A former student of mine who had committed suicide at the age of twenty-three had posted on his website pictures of himself as an infant ("Is this really me?"), of himself as a teenager ("Is this really me?"), pictures of himself as a college student ("Is this really me?") and then a picture of some grains of sand blowing in the wind: ("Then this could easily be me, too.") In his suicide note he asked to be scattered in the desert where his ashes might linger a while on the spikes of cactus plants and glitter briefly in the moonlight.

❁

My husband and I managed to spend the hours till bedtime in separate parts of the house. When we bumped into each other in the kitchen where we took our respective pills every evening, he seemed oblivious to whatever had transpired. Or perhaps, for him, nothing had transpired. We watched the late news, locked the doors, got into bed, turned off the bedside lamps. He said only one thing as we were falling asleep: he took my hand and said, "You take things so to heart. Try to relax. Not everything is the end of the world."

❁

In the morning, I found a place on the living room wall for the desk I had almost owned. A blank piece of wall, where nothing was. where the remnants of a woman's life could have been preserved (also a free and beautiful piece of furniture).

My father had once bought, at an estate sale, some cartons of antiques for his store—in one of them was a leather-bound photo album with an engraved bowl of flowers on the cover. As a child, I had considered the photos: one of a woman in a long skirt, standing with her children in a field of high grass, another in a formal family group: the father sitting, the mother standing beside him, and on his lap, their two little girls in ruffled lacy dresses. I turned page after page, imagining this family's life. My father gave me the album to keep. Over the years, I took it with me whenever we moved. Even now it was still in a box in our garage. I had an impulse to see if I could find it.

The garage smelled of old pool rafts and musty beach towels. Spider webs brushed across my forehead. As I poked about on the shelves I found the set of my grandmother's heavy metal pots (the kind that shared one handle amongst them all). I found the vaporizer I had used when my children had croup. The photo album eluded me but I found a box containing my old maternity dresses. Then I discovered a bag of my children's clothes, which I took into the house.

Who would preserve our family photos? Our daughters? Their children? Who would keep that *other* family's photos after I was dead? Would they someday be tossed into a dumpster like the desk that had been put out in the street? Could we all be put out, in the end, as nothing much?

All morning, my husband remained hidden in his part of the house and I stayed in my familiar place, the kitchen, making his birthday meal: roast chicken and, at the same time, his birthday cake. I pondered the number of birthday candles and decided on one for each decade of my husband's life (seven thick candles) and then a little group of four long skinny candles to equal his age, plus the "one to grow on." Given my state of mind, a generous act, I decided.

Our two daughters arrived at noon. As always in their presence, I felt myself to be in my mid-thirties, the age when I was mothering them, whereas they had bypassed me and become grown women, wives and mothers themselves, professional women, yet I still wanted to tell them certain basic things about getting flu shots and taking calcium. I had to hold my tongue when about to make the simplest of remarks. Any comment could result in a snap of irritation or an argument.

During lunch, while we talked about their children, their children's schools, the cost of college to come, while we ate our roast chicken and baked potatoes, while one of the new CDs of piano music they had brought their father, the waltzes of Chopin, was playing on the music player in the kitchen, I pulled out the bag of children's clothes I had brought in from the garage.

"Girls," I announced. "Look what I found!" I pulled out two matching dresses, toddler sizes 3 and 5, made of pink cotton embroidered with red hearts, with little heart-shaped buttons at the neckline and matching sun hats. "Your twin dresses from when you were little! We got them at Penney's, you were with me, and you each chose these. You wanted to pretend to be twins!" My daughters looked at them with bemused expressions. "Do you remember them?"

"Maybe, I think so."

"I'm not sure."

"But isn't it amazing to think your little bodies were in these clothes, and here they are good as new. You can save them for your granddaughters."

"I don't really want them, Mom. We have so little space in our place."

"I have a son, Mom. He's little. There are no granddaughters in view yet."

"Still, think of the history in these. Think of how cute you looked in them. My utterly beautiful little babies." I handed a dress to each of my daughters. They set them on the table.

"Why not give them to the thrift shop?"

"Or make them into a pillow," the younger added.

Suddenly, I felt tears well up in my eyes, "Daddy did something terrible to me last night."

"*What?*"

"*What do you mean?*"

"I found a beautiful desk in the street that someone had thrown away and I wanted it and Daddy wouldn't let me have it."

They looked at their father. He locked eyes with me as if I had revealed a private matter, betrayed a trust. He bowed his head, resting his forehead against his hand. "I didn't want it here."

"He *refused* to help me get it home."

"Why?" Both girls stared at him.

"Just when we were fixing up our house after all these years, just now when we were making some progress, Mommy wanted to bring this old thing home. Then it would have been here forever."

"But it was beautiful," I said.

"It was dark, we could hardly see it."

"You didn't give it a chance. I could have cleaned it up. We could have decided after we looked at it."

"Once Mommy got it into the house, it would never leave the house," my husband said. "Like everything else that's here."

"Like what?" I demanded. "Like WHAT?"

He looked baffled; then he pointed to the large metal toucan sculpture that I had found in a thrift shop and was now planted on top of the microwave.

"What's wrong with that?" I asked. "I think it's interesting. Unique." My husband and my daughters exchanged glances.

"And what about that?" my older daughter said, pointing to a blue china cow creamer on a shelf—the cow was wearing a cowboy hat.

"These things are unusual," I explained in defense. "I pick up interesting things from yard sales. I paid a dollar for it."

"And that?" my younger daughter pointed to a plaque on the wall that said *God Bless Our Home*. "Since when is that your motto, Mom?"

"It's a nice sentiment. It can't do any harm."

"Or that?" This time she directed me to a mirror hanging over the phone shelf that had the young Elvis's face imprinted on it.

"I didn't appreciate Elvis in my youth," I explained. "I was too young. But I do now. His sexiness and the power of his voice. I'm sorry I never saw him sing in Las Vegas."

"Oh, Mom."

"And what about that thing?" said my younger daughter. They were relentless. She was pointing to a chicken-shaped candle on the counter, whose chicken head was half-melted away.

"That was at my mother's bedside when she was dying," I told them. "Mom-Mom liked it, I'd light up his head with a match and an apple-cinnamon scent would fill the room. She liked it . . . so now I have to keep it. And I hope you girls will keep it after I'm gone."

Suddenly my older daughter began to laugh. "A chicken . . .!" she said, cracking up, "you have to keep a chicken candle!" My other daughter began cackling with glee. "And *we* have to keep a chicken-with-half-a-head candle! Mom, what *is* it with you?" Now my husband was laughing, also. Even I began to laugh. We all looked at the pathetic chicken, really a rooster with his head melted away, and we doubled over with laughter till we were almost crying. I didn't want to laugh as much as I wanted to cry, but in any case, tears were running down my cheeks. My husband offered me his birthday napkin to wipe my face. Then, under the table, he put his hand on my knee and pressed it.

The doorbell rang as we were trying to catch our breaths. We could see a big truck out on the street.

"It's the couch!" my husband said, getting up to open the door.

The old couch came in with a new face. It was a perfect replica of the old couch, with new leather arms where the old and cracked had been, with new fabric (this time a pattern of interlinked brown and white circles where the old had been a brown and white plaid), and with the leather back pillows plump and firm with new down feathers where the old had been squashed and sunken. The seat cushions were renewed to a geometrical plane. The chair and ottoman followed—exactly matched to the couch. The two men, the upholsterers themselves who carried in the furniture, seemed proud and pleased, as if they had invented a miracle that somehow wiped out age and decay.

I waited for my rehearsed hostilities to rise and for accusations to form on my lips: "*My mother and father sat on that couch—and now they're dead! Do you know how much this cost? This furniture will last longer than we can possibly live, it's all your fault, you with your needing 'new' so why not get a new wife, too!*" But none of those words were accessible. And I had no support. After my children had taken their stand, refusing their childhood dresses, I knew upon whose side they stood.

"How beautiful," my daughters said, touching the material on the cushions with admiration, one stroking the perfect couch, the other the chair. "It's just like when they were new," they agreed.

After the men left, with handshakes and a tip from my husband, we sat down on the new furniture. I realized that for perhaps the last ten years, I hadn't actually seen my husband sit down in the living room. Now he was here, on the oldest of all the birthdays of his life, looking confident and content, overseeing his empire: his family and his possessions. He wanted so much for me to be serene and peaceful and I had so often not obliged him. But perhaps now—why not—we could aim for 25,000 nights.

When the phone rang, surely our youngest daughter calling, I stood up from the couch and noticed that I could fairly levitate off the new cushions without asking my husband to grab my hands and pull me up as I had had to do in the recent past. On the old furniture, I had been sinking. From the new, I could fly up, light as a girl.

My Suicides

ON APRIL FOOL'S DAY last year, one of my students, a twenty-three year old young man with a long blond ponytail, sealed his mouth with silver duct tape, put a plastic bag over his head, and managed to make himself die.

"The self has gone away and all the atoms are seething," he wrote in his suicide note, left on his website along with a photo of himself shown vaguely in shadow inside a screened window, his form already fading into the ether.

"Please don't cage it in a box and weigh it down with polished granite. Cremate it. And don't save the ashes in some silly container . . . toss them on the desert . . . I want to be a cactus next!"

His website offered a number of personal notes to his friends, many of his poems and paintings as well as the only story he had ever written (for my class) on the strength of which, he told me at our conference, he wanted to quit school and become a writer. We sat that afternoon in my windowless office on the campus and discussed his future. He had read his story, titled "Generation X," to our class the week before. All my students were nervous about reading their stories aloud; sometimes their voices trembled or the pages in their hand shook

My student's story was about drugs. Our class members were not surprised or even remotely disturbed by this: most of their own stories had to do with drugs and sex. His story involved a group of college friends who spend a few days hiking in the mountains and taking drugs. "Finally, the damn sun's gone. I'm trying to make my eyes as soft as I can . . . Little blue butterfly . . . carry me back to the clover fields of my childhood . . . taste it dissolve, the universe will soon be smooth again, no prickly dried blood clogging every pore. Why did you give us this shit, Timothy Leary?" In the last line of the story, my student wrote: "He rolls over and looks up into the valley: the distant mountains are bathed in early morning gold, a white veil of fog hanging before them: the promised land. Turning to Justin and pointing through the veil, he says, with a twinkle: 'Let's go there.' "

Where, exactly, my student's hero wanted to go did not seem ominous to me until the dean phoned me one morning and told me my student was dead. He had dropped out of school and had given away many of his belongings to his friends and told them he was moving to Santa Cruz to become a writer. He had told me, when he discussed quitting school, that he wasn't worried about making a living. He could work part time for his food. As for lodging, he still had keys to the lab and he could always sleep there. I had told him, as I felt I must, all the reasons he should not drop out of school: you can't count on making a living as a writer, science is a more reliable field than literature. A life devoted to art is about as certain as the lottery.

"I know all that, of course," he said to me, pulling his hand down the length of his pony tail. Had I been twenty again, I could have fallen in love with this young man, a gentle soul who wore his torment in his eyes, a physically beautiful boy—delicately graceful, blue-eyed, tall and slender. Of his farming family across the country, he said "My parents don't know anything about me. They can't figure me out."

After our talk, he offered me his hand. His fingers were cold and damp. I wished him luck; I told him to be sure to stay in touch with me. A few days later, I passed a grassy knoll on campus and saw him stretched out, his hands behind his head, staring at the blue sky. He caught sight of me and sat up, guiltily. I smiled and nodded my appreciation, envying his youth, his poetic trance, his dreamy face turned to the sun. Not so long after, I had the phone call that told me he had killed himself and transformed his seething atoms into ashes for the cactus plants in the desert.

An informal memorial service was held for him on campus a month later. I and two of his other teachers spoke about him. A number of his friends were sprawled on the grass near the student center. His drawings and paintings had been taped to a nearby wall.

I told the students not to romanticize his death; I told them suicide was not a courageous act, and in his case was a waste. I said what I had to say—but I felt Hamlet's conundrum was at the podium with me. My student's friend stood and spoke about religion and Jesus, and how being born again helped him to understand the meaning of life and death and how he loved the lost young man more than ever now and knew he would see him again in the presence of God. I was sorry that someone else, another science student, didn't dispute or argue this in any way.

After the service, the registrar, who was my friend, came up and told me she was glad I took a tough line, not showing pity or admiration for this kind of death. We shared chips and guacamole dip with the others, and afterward looked at my student's paintings as if we were in an art gallery. One painting was of an enormous eagle with a beady eye who has, balanced on his rounded head, a tiny observatory. My student had clearly been making fun of man's puny attempt at "seeing" versus the deep black eye of the true seer.

My very earliest suicide was Tante Iphiga's daughter, Bertha. She killed herself on Easter Sunday when I was eleven years old. I was sitting on the front stoop of our house in Brooklyn, watching the Christian families walk to church—especially the girls in their black patent leather Mary Janes and ruffled dresses and big straw hats with ribbons streaming down the back. I envied girls who had been lucky enough to be born to a family that celebrated Easter. Jewish families had a few big holidays, but not one was as colorful and festive as this. In my mind I was humming Bing Crosby's rendition of "In Your Easter Bonnet . . . " when I was called inside the house and told that something serious had happened to our cousin Bertha—so serious that she was dead.

I remember trying to adopt a pained demeanor—I didn't know Bertha, and I wanted to stay outside and envy the pretty dresses of the girls in the Easter parade. (Bertha was the daughter of my grandmother's brother and his wife with the strange name of Tante Iphiga.) All I knew about Bertha was that she had been dropped on her head as a baby, and was never quite right after that. She secretly married an Italian and continued to live at home till her mother found her wedding band in a box of her sanitary napkins. She went to live with the Italian who treated her badly. He didn't want children, so she began to raise pigeons on the roof of her apartment.

When I was grown up, I learned what sketchy facts the family knew of her life. The Italian husband had a violent temper. He liked to go to big family weddings and funerals. Bertha liked to stay home with her pigeons. On her last Easter Sunday, he went off without her to a wedding. She stuffed towels under the doorframes and around the windows, put the cat outside, turned on the gas, and killed herself. As a child I could see that this suicide caused everyone great distress. No one knew whether to feel sorry or angry, sympathetic or disgusted. They wondered if they could have been kinder to Bertha. She had a hard life. She wasn't pretty. No one in the family ever visited her. I wished I had visited her and seen her pigeons. I was sorry she had married a cruel husband. And I was sorry she had ruined my Easter.

When I had been married for twenty-two years and had three children of my own, my brother-in-law tried to make me an accomplice to his suicide. My sister was hiding with her two sons in a battered women's shelter. Their #1 rule was "You may not call your batterer or abuser." Unable to reach my sister, he called me dozens of times a day, threatening to kill me and my family if I didn't tell him where my sister was, threatening to kill himself if I didn't get my sister to call him back within the next five minutes. Each time he called me, I turned on the tape recorder so I could later play his pleas to my sister, to keep her informed and partly to defend myself against being the only arbiter of his fate. When he called, he pled his arguments to *me*, made his bargains with *me*, declared his love for my sister to *me*, knowing that one way or another this information would get back to her.

When I was home alone, I carried mace in my pocket. I hid the sharp knives in a hall cabinet out of his sight, but easy for me to reach in case I was forced to defend myself. I watched the street from behind my closed blinds in case he might be hiding in wait for me or my daughters. Twice he followed me in his car as I drove on my errands. He knew that sooner or later I would have to visit my sister, and then he would find her.

The police could not help me. They said a crime would have to be committed first before they could pick him up. A man sitting quietly in his car on a public street was not a criminal. When he called and begged me to invite him to dinner, I forced myself to remember the violence he had already done at his home, pounding his head through a wall in anger, biting his baby son on the scalp like an enraged animal. He had pulled a table to pieces, he had thrown a toilet seat at my sister because she wouldn't agree to sell the house so he could buy options on gold futures. When the price of gold went up and he blamed her for losing their fortune, he threatened her life, reasoning that death could not be worse than what they were already going through.

And I, in my quiet home, with my children and my good husband, in my measured and reasoned life, became an accomplice to his fury, to his grief—and I was filled with fear.

One Saturday night, while my husband and daughters and I were having dinner, he called and said if I didn't get my sister on the phone to him in the next ten minutes, he would be dead. This time, he said, he meant it. He knew just how to do it and he was going to do it. I begged him not to, that things would work out, that if only he would agree to have counseling, medication, he could come out of this—but just then my husband came up behind me and took the phone out of my hands. "Don't bother us anymore," he said. "Don't call here anymore. If you want to kill yourself, then just do it. But don't bother us." He hung up.

My children stared at him as if he had pulled the trigger himself. I began to shiver. I called my sister at the shelter and told her what her husband had said. She was sick then, with high fever. Her voice was as hoarse and deep as a man's. *I'll call him*, she said. *I'll tell him I love him. Because I do.*

Five minutes later she called me back to say no one had answered the phone at the house. She said she was too sick to care. She said she was going back to bed and cover her face with a blanket.

On Monday morning, I went shopping for food. No one had heard from my brother-in-law since the call on Saturday night. With my groceries in the car, I was driving across a street that went over a wash, a long corridor coming down from the mountains in which rainwater ran to the sea. In the wash I saw a family of peacocks. A peahen, dun-colored, drab, and her two chicks were walking slowly in the shallow rivulets of water and matted leaves. They seemed lost and confused. They walked first to one side of the wash, then the other. It was hard to imagine how they had got in there, or how they would get out. My eyes were searching in vain for the peacock, the male with his bright colored fan of feathers, his shimmering energy, his beauty. But he was not there.

When I got home, I was carrying bags of food in from the car when the phone rang. My brother-in-law's sister told me that police had found him dead in his car, parked in a far corner of the top level of a parking garage, the hose of the vacuum cleaner attached to the exhaust pipe and coming in the rear window. He had been dead probably since Saturday. At the house police found his insurance policy flung on the floor just inside the door of the living room so my sister would find it there, his final message of fury and revenge.

The fourth of my suicides was a woman my own age, a well-known author of teenage novels, a woman who—as they always say of people who seem to have it all—"had everything to live for." She had a successful career, a devoted husband, and two beautiful children. Her record of publications and sales would be the envy of any writer. She lived in a fine apartment in New York City and she wrote a new book every year from October 1st to October 31st. Her rule for herself, which she told me about, was this: "You must write ten pages a day or you will be shot." I admired her industry. She chose October in which to write her novel because it was a bleak month. Her children were in school, there was no sun in the sky, she wrote all morning every morning, and every afternoon went to a movie by herself. The books she wrote each October were her young adult novels; later in the year she would also write a for adults. Once a book was finished, there was the excitement of selling it, usually for a good deal of money. She was brave in treating subjects for young people: unmarried sex (a divorced parent having a love affair), a mixed-race romance, a boy who chooses to raise the baby his pregnant girlfriend wants to abort, and, later in her career, euthanasia, the killing of an ailing grandparent by the heroine's father—out of mercy. My friend's books were often removed from library shelves; she fought against censorship and traveled to speak out against it. We began writing to one another after our mutual agent died and we were both seeking a new agent. She gave me advice, personal and professional. She held back no secrets—she talked about money the way adults usually don't, telling me about the exact amount of her own earnings, about her husband's, about the advances she knew had been given to other writers. She spoke of secrets, of hers, her husband's and her children's. Without guilt, she read their diaries and letters. I was not so candid, I had a sense of boundaries she did not seem to have, which was also why I wrote with relative caution and she wrote so freely and bluntly. Once, when she came to visit me, I picked her up at the airport. On the way to my house, she began telling me the plot of a novel she planned to begin in October. As she talked with obvious excitement, we passed a burning house. Fire trucks were arriving, their sirens blasting. Smoke was pouring from the windows of the house, and people were gathered across the street to watch. My friend didn't even seem to notice the spectacle, her mind was somewhere else, her brain filled with the images of her book-to-be, her fantasies stronger than the burning reality at hand. During our visit, we talked for three days, stopping only to eat and sleep briefly. But mainly she talked and I listened. She was bursting with talk, her head was under enormous pressure from her visions and her ideas. Her daughters, like mine, were adolescent girls. We spoke about their new sexuality, how we dealt with it, what we feared from it. And she told me she had taken her daughters to see a pornographic movie—that they might as well be exposed to such films in her presence as be shocked by them later, without her there to explain things. I was the one shocked—I was frightened that she wanted to control their minds to that extent, that she felt it was her duty to initiate them personally into aspects of life that were not her business.

When I visited her in New York, she gave me a blanket for my bed made out of the ties of her dead father who had been a psychoanalyst. She told me she was his angel of perfection—that she could do no wrong in his eyes. She confessed that after he died, she tried to kill herself, but had failed. She said it perkily, as if that had been just a mistake, over and done with. One wall of her library was filled with the books of Virginia Woolf who was her heroine and inspiration. She told me that any woman who came after Woolf and wrote a book was already defeated: Virginia Woolf had done the best that could ever be done. And died with stones in her pocket in the River Ouse at the age of fifty-nine.

We wrote letters to one another for fifteen years. Hers were single-spaced, four or more pages long, answered the minute she received mine, as I answered hers. What we had was a fevered long-distance conversation, two women typing madly at opposite ends of the country, consoling one another's literary disappointments, encouraging one another's ideas and plans.

In the library, one day I read a devastating review of my friend's newest adult novel, a book about a woman who had been in a mental hospital for a year, and I was astonished by the casual cruelty of the review, the way the reviewer had tossed out bombs of viciousness. A few days later, at lunchtime (I was frying kosher hot dogs in a pan, their grease was sizzling and spattering burning droplets on my hands) the phone rang and a woman whose voice I had never heard told me she was a friend of my friend and had some bad news for me.

"When did she kill herself?" I cried out, and the woman, who was prepared only to tell me my friend had been sick and died (the newspapers said, a few days later, that her death was caused by "septic poisoning") had to concede that she had "taken something" and was on a respirator for ten days before she died. I berated myself. I should have known something was wrong because no letter had come for more than a week. And like all survivors of suicide, in the after-knowledge of the death, I knew I hadn't called early enough or soon enough—hadn't really cared enough or been alert enough.

"She was only fifty," the woman told me. Perhaps, like Virginia Woolf, my friend had chosen to escape her torment and by-pass old age.

When I flew to New York for the funeral, I stayed with my friend's mother, a woman in her eighties who lived in a huge apartment near Central Park. The walls were filled with clippings of my friend's reviews, photos of her, framed awards, and snapshots of her two daughters. Together her old mother and I took a bus to the church where a gathering of writers and editors sang praises to my dead friend. Her husband told me afterward she had called him at work and told him she'd "done something." He asked her if she had taken pills (he admitted to me he had been hiding her pills for the last few months). He assured her he was calling paramedics and would be right home. He later learned from the paramedics that when they arrived at her door, she opened it and told them there must be some mistake, it wasn't her, look at her, she was just fine. And so they left. Her husband was caught in traffic in Central Park. My friend actually went down to the lobby to get her mail (writers must always get their mail) before she collapsed. By the time her husband arrived home and called the paramedics a second time, she was comatose. Her family buried her at the edge of a river, with a stone on which was engraved "Beauty mysteriously unfolding."

My mother's sister, an old woman, didn't quite achieve her suicide but left enough bloody fingerprints on the phone, enough blood on the sink beside the double-edged razor blade, and pools of it in the bed and on the floor, to convince me it was a real act and not, as her psychiatrist told me later, just a "cry for help." However, my aunt did call me a half-hour after she slit both her wrists and the vein in the crook of one elbow to ask me where she should hide her diamond ring: she didn't want the "crooks here to get it." When I first picked up the phone, her voice was low: "Merrill, I'm tired of living," she said. I said, as I did every day, sympathetically, "I know. I understand how much you miss Uncle Moe, but there's nothing you can do about it but wait and hope your feelings will improve," and she said "There is something I can do. I already did it." "You did what?" "I slit my wrists. Don't call anyone."

I stopped to think hard. I actually considered doing as she asked. I had watched my uncle die of lung cancer. I had seen the colored marks on his chest where the radiation was aimed, seen him unable to swallow because of his charred esophagus, seen the purple bleeding holes on his ankles, seen him gasping for breath under the oxygen mask in the hospital. I had also visited her a hundred times since her widowhood, sat with my aunt on her living room couch in the retirement home with the other old crones, smelled their smell as we all crowded into the small elevator to go down for the watered soup and canned peas for lunch. Why call for help and bring her back to that and the rest of it—her own decay, her inevitable stroke, her broken hip, her feeding tube (all of which I'd witnessed with my mother). These thoughts passed through my mind as I held the phone, and then I saw my husband walk by the doorway of my office and I blurted out: "It's my aunt, she's slit her wrists and doesn't want me to call paramedics."

"You have to," he said simply.

So I called the paramedics. My action was responsible for her ambulance ride, her ten-day lock up-in the mental ward of the hospital, the counseling with other crazies, a roommate who peed on the floor of their room at 2 am. During that period, I had to go to her retirement home and clean up the blood, asking myself every second (as I threw away all her scissors, knives, pins, razor blades and screwdrivers) if I shouldn't have let her bleed to death and be done with it. Now we were all in for it—more old age, more grief, and death anyway.

We moved her to another retirement home and she went on living and regretting that she hadn't done a better job with the razor blade.

A long time ago I took a job on a suicide hotline after six weeks of training. Their office was in a double locked room in an unused wing of a small local hospital. The room was tiny—one chair, a desk, a phone, a teapot, a few paperback novels. Someone had taped up a list of specific instructions to tell the callers: Make yourself a peanut butter sandwich. Put on a sweater. Promise me you'll do what I'm telling you and call me back in fifteen minutes when you are calmer and tell me exactly where you live. We can help you. I swear you won't always feel this way.

Each time the phone rang, I felt a shiver and the hairs on my arms stood up. "My husband knocked out my two teeth and won't let me get them fixed. He doesn't want me smiling at other men. He won't let me out of the house. I found his gun. I'm going to use it."

"Make yourself a peanut butter sandwich," I would say. "Tell me your address."

"I'm a sixty-year-old man with stomach cancer. I weigh 84 pounds. I'm in terrible pain and I have no family. I know a place where I can jump off the roof."

"Put on a sweater," I would say. "Pour yourself a glass of milk and promise you'll call me back and give me your address."

Usually, they never called back. I scanned the newspapers the next day to see if anyone had jumped off a roof or shot herself. If I did get someone to confess his address, I would have the emergency team sent out. I wasn't allowed to ask the outcome of their rescue.

Often, in that little locked room, I got obscene phone calls. The same man called night after night. I began to welcome his calls, sensing the man's obvious enjoyment of life. "I'm picturing you without clothes. I'm doing it right now as I talk to you, honey. Unbutton your blouse for me."

"Do it all you want," I would say, "as long as you don't kill yourself. Call me back when you're done and I'll refer you to a place that can help you."

After my brother-in-law's suicide, I accompanied my sister to a meeting of Survivors-Of-Suicide. We met in a shabby building in the city's downtown area and sat on torn vinyl chairs, eating packaged cookies and holding cups of tea. Everyone told his story, the parents of the teenage boy who hung himself, the daughter of the old man who—standing in the woods behind his house—shot himself in the mouth, the brother of the girl who put poison in her coffee and left a sign on the stairwell saying: "Beware if you enter. Danger! Cyanide inside."

The facilitator told us to try to see our guilt for what it was, helplessness in the face of an unimaginable mystery, and to absolve ourselves. "We who choose to live can never really understand why the person we love chose to die."

We all were asked to describe the thoughts that haunted us. Each person described his special memory: the knock of the police at the door, the endless ringing of a phone when the loved one should have picked it up, the baffling suicide note, the image of the locked car in the garage with a person slumped in the seat. My sister described the sight of the presents her husband had wrapped and left for her on the kitchen counter before he fled the house to kill himself.

I, who was just a visitor there, declined to take my place with the other family members to describe my recollections. Though my suicides lived in me, I did not belong in this first rank of loss. Privately, I saw my brother-in-law on my doorstep, begging to be let in. I saw him alone in his cold and dark house without his family, frantically calling me. But what I thought of most often was the sight of the puzzled peacocks, the pea-hen and her lost chicks, in the high-walled wash that wove its way downhill under the city streets and under the homes of happy families and to the sea.

Why I Must Give Up Writing

IRST LET ME SAY I've been a dedicated writer for half a century. I've published twenty-five books, and I've even won some prizes. I know a real writer is supposed to write for the art itself, yearning only toward self-expression and the joy of creation, ignoring the fickle heart of the market place. I know all about papering the office walls with rejections. I'm not a quitter, not a crybaby (though I have cried a few times and once I crept into bed for a few weeks till a certain violent literary shock wore off). Looking back on my writing life, I see that some warning moments stand out.

In 1967, when my first novel, *An Antique Man*, was published, Joyce Carol Oates wrote: "I'll be reviewing your novel for the Detroit News, and I'll send you a clipping . . . " Three months later she wrote again: ". . . it is a most moving and painful novel, beautifully done, and I will retain certain scenes in my mind for a long time. If the long newspaper strike in Detroit ever comes to an end, I will certainly review the novel."

I don't know when the strike came to an end, but there was never a review. There were other hints to me about the nature of the writing life. William Shawn, at the *New Yorker*, read *An Antique Man*, and wrote to me that he and his staff had tried hard to find a section to stand on its own but they hadn't succeeded. Two months later, one of his staff wrote me: "Mr. Shawn can't get your book out of his mind, so please send it back to us so we can try again to find an excerpt that will work."

Again, I took the trip to the post office with my manuscript. Some weeks later Mr. Shawn sent back the novel a second time. He was sorry, he had tried very hard, but he just couldn't find a section to stand alone. The second rejection was much worse than the first—a kind of brutal blow to the delicate strand of hope that had been fluttering in my mind.

Modern psychology tells us that when a relationship feels wrong, we'd do well to focus on a single issue that's manageable—not to list all the old insults, failings and faults of the beloved. But the list of the failings of my beloved art continues to grow longer. I feel I can no longer live with them.

Recently, I found a letter from a publisher written to me in 1986. "Thank you for sending me your novel. I think you would have to be dead not to think this manuscript is funny and lively. The only problem with it is a certain lack of discipline . . . "

For four months I worked to insert certain disciplines the editor felt were essential. Then she wrote again. "I think that your revisions are excellent, and that you have successfully integrated the fantastic and the real. However, difficulties arise after our heroine leaves the hospital. So now what? Can I say to you that I think you have aimed your plot in a misguided direction? I don't know if I can, but I certainly think so. If these very real difficulties can be resolved we can discuss a book."

What difficulties did she mean? How was I to guess at them? We had no further discussions and my novel was never published.

In 1989, an editor from Little Brown wrote me about my longest novel, a 650-page family saga called *The Victory Gardens of Brooklyn*: "I found this novel to be wonderfully engrossing, full of the marvelously realized characters whose personalities propel them into their individual predicaments. But midway through the manuscript, I felt that the chronological sequence precluded the sort of definable story line that would give each character's subplot satisfying form and substance. If you decide to rework the novel, I would very much like to read it again."

Rework 650 pages? On speculation? With no contract? All the while trying to guess what the editor's vision might be? I wrote, asking if she could be more specific. Well, she could not really point the way for me. I'd have to figure it out for myself. But I had already figured out the way the book should be constructed, that's what had taken me several years of work. I put the book in the closet where one day I listened in to be sure its heart had stopped beating.

The *New Yorker*, after publishing two of my stories, returned a story set at a family Thanksgiving dinner and told me the problem with it was that it was told in present tense. I rewrote it in the past tense and sent it back. Apparently, they had second thoughts. "It turns out to be one of those common family event stories. We have too many of these in our inventory."

An editor at *Esquire* asked me to revise a story three times, then gave up on it saying, "Sorry, but less is more." An editor at *Redbook* "loved" a story up to the point where the narrator, who is depressed, decides to consult a therapist. The *Redbook* editor felt that that therapy might suggest insanity to some of their readers. "What should I have her do, go to Italy instead?" I asked, and the editor said that would be perfect. I made the changes and *Redbook* published the story.

In the 1990s, I sent my novel *King of the World* to twenty-five publishers. The letters of response to it showed real visceral distress: "This book is so powerful it reminds me of spoiled meat," and "This makes me very uncomfortable to read, how do you know how men think?" It was one of the early novels about domestic violence, and all the female editors said of the heroine, "Why doesn't she just leave him?" Finally, an editor at Atlantic Monthly Press sent me a letter saying he felt the novel was stunning and he wanted to publish it. However, he had to get support from each of five other editors. The process took five months. Each month he would write me that Editor Two loved it and it was now going to Editor Three or Editor Four. I hardly left the house. I kept the phone free for a possible call from the press. Then I learned that Editor Five also loved it. Editor Six now had the manuscript. I was unable to sleep. I had heart palpitations. I couldn't eat. And then I got the final letter. Editor Six said it was very impressive but he didn't see how they could market it.

That was the time I took to my bed. For some weeks I was ill. Cynthia Ozick suggested I send it to Pushcart Press, which did not have six editors, but one man, Bill Henderson, in charge of the decisions. Bill chose to publish the book and gave it the Pushcart's Editors' Book Award. The reviews made me hopeful. *Publishers Weekly* wrote, "A mock coronation opens this brilliant novel about the harrowing but erotically charged 15-year marriage of Ginny and Michael." Bill Henderson called me and said, "I think it's going to happen. New American Library wants to do a mass market paperback." But somehow it didn't happen. I never learned why. And what does it matter, since we all know "almost" doesn't count.

I had a number of agents, all of whom worked in my behalf. One finally urged me to "put a little more sunshine in your typewriter," and another fired me, saying she could earn more money by selling cookbooks.

My last six books have been published by university presses, which, once peer reviewers give approval, blessedly leave the author to his vision and his architecture.

For twenty-five years I applied for NEA and Guggenheim grants. The Guggenheim turn-down letter always came on my birthday, March 15th. I gave up applying when I realized I had asked four esteemed persons each year to write about my impressive qualities. A hundred letters! And all for naught. On the twenty-sixth year, I wrote this letter to the Guggenheim Foundation on September 20, 1994:

I am a 56-year-old writer who has applied for a Guggenheim grant for the last 25 years Each year I have dutifully and scrupulously filled out the forms, written apologetic beseeching requests to my references, and sent your committee the required "narrative essay" of my projected plans and my list of publications. Many of my references—those who taught me, those who supported me—are now dead or are too old to refer me. Wallace Stegner died last year at the age of 84. Andrew Lytle is 92 years old. Milton Hindus is not well. George Core, editor of The Sewanee Review, *has explained that he (he!) has felt snubbed by your refusal to award me a grant and thus will not write again. Norma Klein is dead. Lynne Sharon Schwartz is recovering from the Epstein-Barr virus. Alice Adams, I am told recently, had cancer surgery. Cynthia Ozick has written for me for at least the last eight years. She and Bob Stone, my classmate in the Stegner fiction workshop at Stanford in 1962, are lately overwhelmed by requests to appear and receive literary prizes and honors.*

How can I ask them to write for me again, merely to insist one more time that I am a talented writer who deserves a grant—for what other content can be found in these letters? Let me save all of them the trouble this year. Allow me not to cringe with embarrassment in order to beg their favors one more time. Let me not beseech these illustrious and absorbed artists who would—out of friendship and obligation and goodwill—take time out of their dwindling years to write the required form letter to Guggenheim.

Please accept instead this reference letter from me or kindly consult the 100 letters sent to you in my behalf in the past 25 years. This letter is to state that I have published fourteen novels and four volumes of short stories, I have won major literary prizes, I have lived the dedicated life of a serious writer, I have suffered the requisite years of rejection and I have seen enough turn-down letters to kill a horse, letters which for some reason arrive every year on my birthday, March 15th. Their annual message urges me to understand that, as always, "a large number of excellent candidates had to be denied." The Guggenheim committee and I have been writing the same letter to one another for 25 years. This year I find I must alter the nature of the exchange. Enclosed is a comprehensive narrative of my life as a writer. Please consider me for a grant before the year of death finds occasion to be added after my name.

What does it all mean? Is the writing life all about luck, or about talent, or about plain accident? Should a writer hope for posthumous comfort? When I told one of my daughters that I was tired of "begging and being bludgeoned," she said, "Those are violent words, aren't they?" But when a writer has given away great chunks of her life, and all her understanding of it, and all her knowledge of it, when she has risked losing friendships and the love of family members, when she has typed ten million words (but never had a job as a typist, never had a real income, never will have a pension), when her books are published but often not reviewed and even less read, and when she finds that bitterness is overtaking hopefulness, isn't it time to stop?

I think I've written all I want to say. I did want to write this.

The Harpsichord on the Mountain

ECAUSE MY HUSBAND had some years earlier taught in Florence for his university, we decided to return and live there *senza gli studenti* for a month to see the city on our own. My husband, who was a lover of early music and who had built his own harpsichord many years before, had been urged by his musical friends to look up a famous North American harpsichordist who lived in Florence. The man was known to have several rare historical instruments, and had been cordial to other amateur players from the US who had visited him there. We took his phone number with us but I knew it would take time for my husband to get up the courage to call him; he could not be rushed in such matters.

We did though, as soon as we were settled in our apartment, visit the workshop of a restorer of old instruments. She was a gracious woman who welcomed us into one of those crumbling streetfront doorways and led us through passageways of ancient stone till the hallway opened out into a brightly lit workshop where two other women were bent over harpsichords and pianofortes. Adjoining the workshop was an elegant but small concert hall whose walls were covered with photographs of Bach. The owner gladly showed us her instruments in progress and she, too, urged my husband to call this famous player who lived near Porta Romana and who relished showing his collection to knowledgeable players.

We had many other things we wanted to do in Florence. My husband knew more Italian than I did, but I could manage the basic needs of shopping for food (*"Quatro piatte prosciutto cotto, per favore"*) and clothing (*"Posso avere un po' de sconto?"*).

With the help of a friend who knew an agent, we had rented two rooms in the Palazzo Pucci, a five-hundred-year-old apartment house on Via Ricasole in *il centro* of Florence. If I looked out our third floor living room window to the left, I could see the bell tower of the Duomo two blocks away. To the right was the Accademia where Michelangelo's *David* was perched on a pedestal so high that in order to see his face one had to focus first upon his genitals and then look upward.

The day we visited the Accademia, a girl fainted from the apparently unbearable beauty of the statue above her. A chair was brought for her, and her companion (a much older man), stood behind her chair and from time to time patted her face. Each time she opened her eyes and raised them to David's face, she'd swoon again, her eyes rolling up into her head. Her companion continued to hold her face between his hands. For a moment I had a desire to swoon against my husband and have him bring me to. I'd read about this fainting syndrome, common in Florence, caused by an excess of art and beauty, but I'd never experienced it. If I stayed too long in a museum, I would get hungry and begin to imagine an Italian pizza, uncut on a plate, thin crusted, perhaps "*quatro stagione*" or "*prosciutto e funghi*," and art would flee from my mind.

Though we'd been jubilant at the location of our rooms, we'd forgotten that any apartment overlooking a street in the center of Florence would constantly be filled with the deafening buzz and roar of Vespas. At certain hours the noise reached such levels that my husband and I could not speak to one another without shouting.

"How do Italians stand it?" I screamed to him. He was sitting in the enormous living room about three inches from the television, trying to improve his Italian by listening to a quiz show. He didn't hear me. He had a blanket over his head. It was nearly the end of October and the weather was turning cold. Italians did not use heat in their homes till November 1st unless an emergency weather situation called forth a decree from the government. I was sitting at an antique desk wearing my sweater and my coat. I was trying to type on my computer, but my fingers were too chilled to move accurately over the keys. I didn't know yet if I was enjoying myself in Italy, although when I sent e-mails home, I thought it sounded impressive to write our grown children: *"We are living in a palace with 17th century oil paintings of the Pucci family hanging on the walls. Antiques are in every cabinet. The Marchesa Pucci has an office downstairs from which she controls the family empire: textiles, wine, and clothing designed by Emilio Pucci (her famous and dead husband.) The shop right next to this building sells Pucci clothing—-I priced a handkerchief with a Pucci design, it cost $65. God forbid we should spill wine on our Pucci tablecloth; we have signed away our lives to leave everything exactly as we found it."*

Pucci, Gucci, I really didn't know one from the another. At home I shopped in thrift shops, which was a form of entertainment to me. I liked to browse through the items among which other people had lived (and died.) I was not impressed by designer clothes and in fact had a low opinion of the elegant aristocratic Emilio Pucci, who—from what I'd read—was in love with himself and spent too much time away from his young wife having dalliances with other women. From a book I'd read about him at home I had photocopied certain pages in the hope that one day I could have a chat with the Marchesa and show her pictures of herself at her wedding to him, of herself standing on the roof of this very building (with the great Duomo in the background) in the blush of her first love. One photo showed Emilio Pucci mounted on a black steed, imposing and threatening as Mozart's *Commendatore*, in a black velvet cape and black boots about to lead off the first game of *calcio* in the year's soccer season.

The Marchesa —now a woman of about sixty—was guarded by two employees—one a bull-dog faced matron, and the other an eighteen-year-old beauty named Sabrina with blonde hair falling in delicate tendrils about her Botticelli-like face. These women worked in an office on the first floor of our building. The Marchesa worked in another office opposite theirs. I knew that at the sound of the *ascensure* coming down from the floors above (those freezing rooms which the Marchesa rented to Americans for astronomical prices), Sabrina and the bull-dog woman would rush into the hall to prevent anyone from attempting to walk into the garden at the rear of the house and thus pass the open door of the Marchesa's office. We lived in fact in a fortress: the front door so thick and heavy I had to turn the key and push the door with my shoulder to enter the inner chamber which was itself like an empty, dimly lit prison cell. To get beyond it, through the floor-to-ceiling bars and to the elevator, I needed a second key. A third key opened our apartment door.

Sabrina, who handled the tenants, knew almost no English, and had to be communicated to via pantomime. I tried to tell her that the pots in our tiny kitchen had no covers. Since all the pots (dented and nearly useless) had metal handles, I needed a potholder. I also needed an extension cord since each room had only one electrical outlet. It was not possible to have light in the living room if the TV was on and the computer plugged in. It was not possible to plug in my laptop if the light and TV were on. The beautiful girl nodded her head and smiled and indicated this would all be taken care of. I had no sense that she understood anything I'd said and when the next day I found a light bulb at my door, I was sure of it.

Our apartment had one huge living room, one small bedroom, one tiny kitchen, and one infinitesimal bathroom—which was at the far end of the living room and seemed to have been carved out of the huge blocks of stone which made up the building. The shower enclosure was of cracked and peeling plaster but the shower handles were gold. There was no shower door or curtain, so that water sprayed all over the floor and walls. The towels were always damp and smelled of mildew. There was no way to get them dry—no heated radiators to hang them over, no clothesline to hang them on. The apartment smelled in general like a dirty dishrag.

I entertained myself much of the time by leaning out the window which opened on Via Ricasole. Across the street, in the third-floor rooms of the opposite building, I could see young women working at computers. On the floor below I always saw the same dark-haired woman sweeping the floors or washing her windows. On the narrow canyon-like street, Italians flew by on their scooters. Women on their way to work wore dress suits and heels and kept their leather purses protected on the floorboards between their legs. Young men in black leather jackets and helmets tore down the street on motors that never knew a muffler. A shop across the street, called "Vice Versa," displayed a window full of brightly colored plastic kitchenware, splashes of orange and yellow and green in the drab, stone-colored street. Often people clustered at the shop window, jostling one another, on rainy days tangling their umbrellas together. They seemed fascinated by the neon-bright juice pitchers, translucent cutting boards, American sized coffee mugs, see-through cutlery. A block away was Michelangelo's *David* but the Italians craved plastic dinner-wear. When I went into the store myself one day, I was shocked at the high prices of their wares. At home, I could buy a plastic pitcher for a dollar in the 99 Cent Store; in Italy, such an item was 40,000 lire, about $28.

I worried about how much money we were spending here. Each time I sent an e-mail on my computer, the *scatti* ticked by (a counter measured how many minutes I used the phone). Someone had told me that if I used the phone before 6:30 in the morning, my charges would be much cheaper. I'd often get up at dawn, run through the freezing living room with a blanket wrapped around my shoulders, sit down at the antique desk, and log-in to my e-mail server. I'd write my daughters the news of the day: "Yesterday evening we had osso buco for dinner and later, as we walked across the Arno we saw a mime on the Ponte Vecchio. He was in draped in a Roman robe, spray-painted silver, and he stood as still as a statue for perhaps fifteen minutes while people came up and dropped coins in the silver bowl at his feet. Then, very slowly, he'd raise his arm, as one waking from the dead, to thank those who made contributions. On our way home, we stopped at a profumeria, where Daddy bought me earplugs. When the girl brought out foam rubber plugs, Daddy asked her if they didn't have something more 'forte' (he indicated the 'motos' going by)—and she found us a box of pink wax ear plugs. We paid $9 for them! I hope they work tonight. Our bed has two blankets on it—one made of wool with a Pucci label on it, and one which seems to be an animal skin of some kind, heavy as lead, with fur on one side, smooth like leather on the other. It smells a hundred years old. A cabinet beside our bed, made of wood, has a pull-out drawer with a chamber pot in it! We are living here in the Middle Ages. Yesterday I hoped to meet the Marchesa and brought down some pages I'd photocopied at home from a book about her. She heard me ask her assistant if I might give them to her and slammed her office door against me. She is clearly not interested in Italian-American relations. I have heard that her life is very sad, that she lost a son in a car accident, and that her heart was broken by the womanizing of her famous husband. I am so lucky to have married Daddy. He can be found every night in front of the TV with a blanket over his head, so I always know where he is."

❁

As a personal protest to the prices in the Pucci shop next door, I took the bus to the outskirts of Florence where we had once lived and where I'd often visited a little "mercato usato"—a thrift shop. A woman was just locking up the shop for the day. I recognized her and called out "Paola!" In a moment she was embracing me, her face alight with welcome. She unlocked the door and invited me in even though the sign on the shop said "Chiuso." Inside, the tiny store was crammed with clothing of every sort, some items hanging up high, some folded in little cubby holes, some piled in plastic baskets and labeled: "Donna." "Uomo." "Pantaloni." "Camici." "Vestiti." Winter coats were 10,000 lire ($7). Everything else was a dollar or two. But on this day she pointed out to me an iridescent blouse hanging in the window, a garment made of a glowing purple knit shot through with silver threads. She took the blouse off the hanger and held it up to me. The label read "Gucci." The real thing! "*Aah, bella.*" She handed it to me. "*Un regalo.*" A gift, for coming to see her. We hugged once more. She stuffed into a bag other presents for me as well: a silk scarf, a leather belt, a sweater with Chinese acrobats embroidered upon it, a battery run radio/alarm clock whose directions, in Italian, I would never decipher. We embraced a final time when I left. I smiled to myself all the way home. I was certain that today I loved Italy. But when the bus control police boarded the bus, locked the doors and demanded to see everyone's tickets in order to catch anyone who was trying to ride free, then I hated Italy.

❁

I returned to the Pucci Palace with my Gucci blouse. That night my husband and I walked to the piazza in front of the Duomo where I bought a piece of jewelry from an Indian tradesman who had set up a stand with bits of glass and tin resembling jewelry. I chose a mother-of pearl (plastic) dolphin on a silver (tin) chain for $3. It matched beautifully the silver threads in the Gucci blouse.

After we had dinner of pesto and wine at one of the trattorias beyond the piazza, we walked to the Lutheran church on the other side of the river to hear a Bach organ concert. We had looked in vain to discover any harpsichord concerts; one was advertised on fliers given out by young women dressed in red velvet gowns on the Ponte Vecchio announcing a medieval costume drama. My husband thought the price was too high for what was not likely to be an authentic performance with historical instruments.

At the organ concert, only a few were in attendance. At the first chords of Bach, I felt the music coming up and into my body through the wooden pews. There was nothing on the walls of the church, no bleeding Christ, no saints under glass, not one gold-leaf pulpit or pieta or burning rank of candles. We heard only Bach's godly music singing through the thundering pipes. The organist sat at a keyboard high above the pews, his back to the backs of the audience. He played as if he were bodiless, or at least as if the body he inhabited were of no consequence to him. When he played the last notes, he took no bows and gave no encores. He disappeared and left just the vibrations reverberating in our bones.

The night was cold when we got out, it had rained. We crossed the Arno over the bridge and paused to watch the street lights ride over the ripples of the current. A couple was kissing a few feet away. There were lovers kissing all over Florence. I had taken a whole roll of film of nothing but lovers kissing, at bus stops, over plates of pasta, outside the *rosticceria*, inside the *gelateria*. I sometimes looked at my husband and wished he would have such an impulse, to kiss me in a public place, but I'd known him since I was fifteen. He wasn't likely to satisfy such a fantasy of mine.

❖

I had a sense, as we approached our doorway on Via Ricasole, that a man was following us, but not on the narrow sidewalk. He was walking slightly behind us in the middle of the street. When we got to our doorway, I put my key in the lock, and at that moment the man darted between the scooters parked on the street and rang the lowest doorbell on the wall just beside me. The street light reflected off his black leather pants. He stood, breathing hard, right behind me. I knew at once he didn't belong there, that the bell he pressed rang only in the Marchesa's office on the first floor and that she nor her workers were ever there at night. This man, I understood in a flash, was going to enter the building as we did and trap us between the locked front door and the locked iron gate beyond it. Either that, or he would follow us into the elevator and rob us upstairs. Or worse. I knew my husband had no inkling of this. He was born without a sense of danger; his mind did not contain normal cautionary apparatus. I astonished him by pulling my key out of the lock, grabbing his arm, and saying loudly, "Let's go and buy a gelato." I dragged him along the street in the direction of the Accademia beyond which was a popular gelateria.

"What?" he said. "Now? So late?" But I was glancing over my shoulder and I saw the man rush away from our door in the other direction. We had narrowly missed something terrible that would have happened to us, and I was shaking at the thought of our hair-thin escape. I didn't want to eat ice cream, but I made us each buy a gelato to take time to be sure the man was gone, and to gather my senses again in the brightly lit shop which always had people in it. "Nocciola"—hazelnut—was the flavor I preferred but now I could not even taste it. I was already shivering, and the gelato made me colder. When I told my husband what had happened, what I had perceived was going to happen, and why we might have just escaped being mugged or killed, he was doubtful. I repeated why I had to be right about this, the late night, the obvious tourists we were, what I'd heard about drug users and their need for money, and how the man couldn't have been visiting anyone in the building at that hour, that the buzzer he rang did not belong to one of the rented apartments, how he had run away when we hadn't entered the building. My husband didn't contradict me, but I knew he didn't believe we had been in danger of our lives. His skepticism and stubborn lack of fear made him seem stupid. Thinking he was stupid frightened me, the thought that I had married a stupid man.

❀

In the Milan train station, we'd nearly been killed because he refused to hail a cab when I asked him to. En-route to Florence, we'd flown from Los Angeles to Malpensa airport and stayed the night in a Milan hotel which had advertised that it was "right across the street from the station." Our plan was to take the train to Florence in the morning.

However, we had four suitcases between us, and the "street" was enormous, with many roadways converging from many angles upon the train station. I argued that we should call a cab and be driven to the closest point to boarding the train. My husband felt we could easily pull our suitcases on wheels, one in each hand, across the many intersections of the busy street. He didn't like to call cabs if he could walk or take a bus. I knew he felt helpless in a cab, at the mercy of the driver who, in some way, had us in his power.

Years before, also in Milan, we had mistakenly parked our rented car in a tow-away zone near a museum. When we came out, our car, with all our luggage (and our traveler's checks) was gone. A cab driver in a café who had overheard us calling the police, offered to drive us to the arena where towed cars were taken and held till a fine had been paid. When we got there, we saw hundreds of cars in rows waiting to be claimed. The cab driver offered to take care of paying the fine for us, to spare us the complications and paperwork. He said the fine would cost $150. My husband hesitated. "Let him do it," I whispered "give him the money, he understands the system here," but he ignored me and told the man he would pay the fine himself. The moment he said this, the cab driver jumped in his cab and sped away without collecting his fare. It took us two hours to find our car, but the fine turned out to be only $15.

❄

When I asked our hotel clerk if a cab could get us close to the trains, he said, yes, a cab would take us around the back of the station and to the level of the tracks. Still, my husband wanted to cross the street by foot. We staggered like drunken sailors toward the station, each of us jerking and hauling our heavy suitcases up and down curbs, pulling or pushing or pulling *and* pushing simultaneously, threatened by speeding cars, our arm sockets nearly torn out by the time we gained the safety of the sidewalk. What presented itself to us then was a new obstacle, a long flight of steps up to the entrance to the station. The words sat on my tongue like a frog: *If we'd taken a cab . . .* I didn't say them since I had the sense to remember where this kind of conversation would lead. We both needed our strength.

My husband told me to stay below and took one suitcase at a time to the top of the staircase, coming back again and again till three were lined up at the top. For a moment I felt he was chivalrous and my heart softened. He looked quite handsome in his raincoat and turtleneck shirt, his hair blowing wildly in the chilly air. Then he took the fourth suitcase in one hand and my hand in his other and helped me up the stairs. In the lobby of the station, we saw there was yet another level to ascend—and this time by escalator. Others already on the escalator were transporting their luggage upward in wire carts on wheels. My husband spotted the source of these carts and, leaving me guarding the suitcases, went away for so long I feared we would miss our train. By the time he came back pushing two carts, I was cursing my luggage, all the shoes and sweaters and dresses so carefully chosen with images of myself "in Italy, appropriately dressed for all occasions." I realized it didn't matter what either of us wore, we weren't being judged for our good fashion sense, and the stuff was literally killing us. I could hardly breathe from pushing my tons of junk around.

We somehow got two suitcases balanced on each wire cart. I tried to push mine forward but it stopped short and the handle crashed into my breasts. My husband showed me that in order for the cart to move, a wire bar under the handle had to be pressed upward. We soon understood the reason for this, since once the cart was pushed onto the escalator, with two wheels on one step and two on a lower step, the wheels locked for safety until the bar was pressed to move the cart forward.

We were moving upward on the escalator when I looked up to see where the ride would end. The level on which we would board our train was a vast distance above us. I drew a deep breath. We had a long moment to rest before we gained the top.

I was looking down at the station floor below when suddenly something happened. The woman ahead of my husband reached the top of the escalator and couldn't move her wagon forward and off the moving staircase. The stairs disappeared from under her and crushed her back against my husband's wagon. He couldn't move forward and fell back against my wagon, which pushed me backward against the person behind me. I screamed and felt myself falling down the escalator. I heard the astonished cries and curses of others behind me who also began to tumble downward as the steps beneath their feet collapsed and the crush of people accumulating at the top pressed them back. I had a sense we were all falling into hell from a height as great as the ceiling of the Sistine Chapel.

I never figured out if the woman at the top found the way to release the brake from her wagon and push it forward or if someone pulled her forcibly off the escalator—but the jam was somehow relieved and my husband was able to get his wagon onto solid land. Whoever pushed me upward to a standing position from behind also shoved me—and my wagon—off the escalator. I was faintly aware of the desperate rush of bodies to escape the folding steps. Everyone was running to save their lives and to catch their trains.

✻

The train to Florence stalled on the track for two hours somewhere midway there. We sat facing an older couple who ate salami slices and talked incessantly to one another. I tried to position my feet between theirs under the narrow table between us. Next to my husband was a girl on a cell phone, who chattered away during the entire trip, laughing even while the train was stalled, and while we were all sweating in the stifling air. A woman in official uniform distributed two dry biscuits wrapped in plastic to each person and, at some point, the conductor passed out certificates which would entitle us to a partial refund of our fare, to be claimed at the Florence station, due to the unscheduled delay in the middle of nowhere.

✻

Toward the end of our stay in Italy, I said to my husband, "Call the harpsichord man. We don't have many days left here. Don't miss this opportunity." I urged him each day, and then one afternoon I saw him at the little desk where the phone and my computer sat. "Yes," I heard him say, "I'm a harpsichord player, just an amateur, but a player. Yes, my wife and I would very much like to do that. Yes. Do you know what bus would take us to Porta Romana? We live near the center. I see. Yes, a cab. But what about a bus? The #12? Yes, I see. Thank you. We'll be there between 7:30 and 8 tonight then. Very good."

✻

I decided to wear my Gucci blouse and my dolphin necklace. The harpsichordist had told my husband we could either take a cab from the Duomo for about 20,000 lire, or take the bus at San Marco to Porta Romana.

"Let's take the cab," I said.

"Let's take the bus. Then we can look around the neighborhood. And after we see him, we can have dinner in the piazza near Porta Romana.

❁

The piazza of the Porta Romana had, in its center, an enormous statue of a woman carrying a marble beam on her head. The beam extended far beyond her head, unbalancing the sculpture and giving me a sense of pain, as if I wanted to unburden her and let her rest.

"We have to find the street next to Via Ugo Foscolo," my husband said, consulting his map, "and then we have to find *numero novantanove.*"

"*Novantanove?*"

"99," he said.

The road began to climb directly from the piazza, a steep road going straight up. We passed "numero 1" and then walked upward for a good distance and passed "numero 3." I was already out of breath. Ten minutes later we passed "numero 4."

I said to my husband, "We want numero 99?"

"It can't be too far," he replied.

I climbed, conserving breath. Darkness was falling fast. We walked another full block to numero 6. At this rate, I realized, we'd have to reach the very top of the mountain to find the harpsichordist's house. Then it struck me that of course he would live on the mountaintop. He was famous. He was living in Italy. He would not have his home in the crowded apartments near the busy and noisy piazza.

The street had narrowed and on both sides were tall stone walls. The houses hidden behind them were very far apart and marked only by solid wooden gates. Night was upon us and cars were speeding past us up the mountain with their headlights on.

"Stand back," I yelled to my husband. "They don't expect anyone to be walking here. They probably can't even see us!"

It was not possible to walk pressed against the wall since there was a culvert or ditch running along the side of the road. We could no longer walk side by side, so my husband stepped ahead of me and took my hand to pull me along. My heart was pounding. My knees were aching with each step along the increasingly steep upward slant of the road. I wanted to tell him: *This is a terrible mistake. We should turn around and go back to the Porta Romana and get a cab.*

We were now only at number 18, then—ten minutes later—number 20. We were already late and should have been at our appointment a half hour ago. It would take us (I guessed) an hour to walk back down to the piazza if we wanted to find a cab. By then the famous man would have presumed we weren't coming. Or by then we'd by lying dead in the road, run over like two stray dogs. My hip was beginning to pain me and, even though I was wearing a jacket, I was beginning to shiver from the cold.

"Watch out!" I screamed at my husband as a car passed by me so close its side-view mirror grazed my body. "My God! We're going to be killed! No one expects people to be on this road. I'm sure *no one ever walks here.*"

"People walk here all the time," my husband said, although there was no one, no one but us, on this dangerous road. I thought about this strange man I was with, about my pledge to cherish and honor him and about the mystery of marriage.

"We're not even a third of the way there!"

"Look up ahead, I think it flattens out," he called back to me. "I think I see a square up there. Then many numbers will be all there altogether in a cluster."

And the road did flatten out. I saw a little red mailbox. I imagined there would be a public phone from which we'd call a cab, maybe a café where we could rest, warm up, drink some coffee. The numbers would, like a prayer answered, leap from 22 to 99, and we would be there at the harpsichord on the mountain. All would end well.

But there was no square there, no cluster of homes, no phone. Just a mailbox at a little curve in the road, and we were back climbing endlessly upward.

"Probably it's just a little further," my husband said, and I hated the way his legs moved forward, toward those harpsichords he wanted to see, on this errand that supplanted everything else in his mind.

"I want to go down the mountain now," I told him. "We're nowhere near his house. We'll never find it. We're *nowhere* near it. *Do you understand that*? He won't be there even if we ever get there." I could see a few distant lights dotting their way up the mountain. No clusters, no inviting places for human beings. "If you don't turn around and come with me, I'll go down myself, without you!" I threatened. But when I thought of going down that steep hill in the dark, alone, past the whizzing cars, I wanted to cry.

"It can't be far," my husband said, and suddenly I stopped and tugged on his hand to make him face me. "Listen! That man is crazy!" I screamed. "He was crazy not to tell you that the bus doesn't go to number 99! He should have said a cab is the *only* way to get there!" Hysteria had taken over my voice, and some kind of witch was talking out of my lips. "You were too cheap to take a cab and look where you've got us! We're going to die here! Be killed! Or freeze to death! You want me to die just so you can see those fucking harpsichords!"

My husband stopped short and faced me. I could see his expression in the glow of approaching headlights. His fists were clenched and he was baring his teeth at me. He looked insane. Suddenly he stamped his feet. I thought he was going to strike me.

"Just come on," he said. "Just keep going. It's the only thing to do."

He took my hand tightly in his and pulled me forward. I looked longingly at the stone walls, imagining that at the next gate, number 30 or 40 or 50, I would bang on the knocker till someone came and let me inside his house, let me sit down and rest, let me get warm. I stepped into the culvert and walked close to the wall. I heard dogs howling. My husband's mother was right when she'd told him thirty-odd years ago that I wasn't the right girl for him. I wished he had listened to her. I tripped on something and went down on my knees.

"Give it up!" I shouted at my husband. "Just give it up!" But this time he would not argue, he just tugged me to my feet and dragged me along, like baggage, like those suitcases he jerked over the road and up the escalator at the Milan train station.

❉

Suddenly there was no wall at the side of the road, no dogs barking, no culvert, and no cars, nothing but a cessation of all signs of life. Ahead was nothing but open field, huge, blank, empty countryside and forest beyond.

"That's it," I said. "We're at the end of the world. There are no more houses." A cold wind came from the woods, hitting us in the face. My husband looked around. Finally, he seemed baffled.

"We'll die here," I told him.

He had nothing to say. We could both see that if we moved forward, we'd move into total blackness, into the wilderness. There were no more cars coming. It was very quiet, but for the wind.

"If another car passes—" I said, "I'm going to stop it."

"Don't do that," my husband said but I already saw headlights in the distance coming up the hill. I was already doing it. I stepped out into the center of the road and waved my arms like a maniac.

I saw myself in the car's headlights, a crazy woman in a Gucci blouse dancing on the road. The car, an old red truck, swerved to pass me by, then slowed down. I began to run toward it. "I'm going with him," I screamed over my shoulder to my husband, "no matter where he's going."

My husband began running after me. The truck stopped and a young man got out and came toward us. I began to babble, "We are lost, we are lost!" but the man, who looked sympathetic, didn't understand me. "*Novantanove*," I cried. "There is no such number but *mio marito*" —(now I found words) —"*mio marito e non logico!*" I now grabbed my husband's arm: "Tell him in Italian! Tell him we're lost and need help."

While the men spoke to one another in Italian, I opened the door of the truck and got inside. I wanted to live in this truck the rest of my life. Sitting down on its lumpy springs was like experiencing a miracle. I wanted to marry the young Italian who owned the tinny truck and ride with him over the crest of the mountain and live with him in some farmhouse and *never* go back to the Palazzo Pucci with the insane stranger, my husband, who had snarled at me when I was exhausted and afraid. I didn't want to be alone with him in that freezing tomb of a place under the vicious, aristocratic faces of the Pucci ancestors.

The driver of the truck got back in beside me, and my husband squeezed in from the passenger side door. "He doesn't think there are any more houses ahead, but I told him we're only at 23 and we need number 99. He said to get in we'd see what's up ahead."

The truck started up and we drove forward into the black forest. Nothing lit the road but his headlights. The truck smelled of grease and the young man's body. "*Grazie, Grazie,*" I said to him over and over. I could feel his hip against mine. My husband tried to take my hand, but I shook him off.

We drove for miles, further and further from the Porta Romana where the crazy woman stood in the middle of traffic wearing a girder on her head.

"*Ecco*," the man said. And then we saw some lights, and then we saw a wall, and then we saw a door. The truck slowed and pulled toward the wall.

"*Novantanove!*" my husband cried jubilantly. "This is it!"

He got out and pulled me after him. I wanted to give the young man all our money, the pearly dolphin around my neck, my Gucci blouse off my back. My husband reached for his wallet, too. But the man smiled, dipped his head at me, "*Signora*," he said, "*Grazie, no.*" He shook my husband's hand warmly and drove off in his truck.

✤

The famous harpsichordist came to the ring of the bell, this lunatic person who had not told my husband that no one should ever try to take a bus to this place. The man was tall, stately, dignified, handsome. Fame and money had got him a home on a mountaintop. My husband was not famous or rich, and we lived in a plain house on a flat street. Luck, I felt, was truly unevenly distributed among human beings.

"We *walked* here from the Porta Romana," I accused the man. "You didn't tell my husband we'd have to walk up a mountain."

"I did mention to him it was best to take a cab."

"Well," I said. "He thought it best not to."

"Why don't you both come in?" he said, leading us through an open courtyard and into his villa, up a narrow staircase into a room with a high domed ceiling, tile floors, and a harpsichord on each wall. I found a small bench and sat down at once. The famous man was telling my husband that the villa was built in the "quattrocentro" and he had many difficulties in remodeling it. He said something about grown children in the US and I wondered who lived here with him now, if anyone.

"Go ahead," he told my husband. "Try any of these instruments you like. This one is a Dowd, this square one is a Dutch style virginal, a Skovroneck, and this is a genuine Stein fortepiano like the kind Mozart used, it's from about 1796." I didn't bother to look at the instruments, I had seen enough harpsichords to last me all my life, but said to him, "Aren't you going to play them a little for us?" The man needed to understand the sacrifices we had made, the distance we had come and the dangers we had faced to get here. In spite of my personal problems with my husband, I felt he should get what he had envisioned.

The harpsichordist simply shrugged, smiled condescendingly, turned his back and disappeared down the stairs. His message seemed clear: *I play for money. Buy a ticket if you want to hear me perform.*

My husband wandered around the room, sitting down to play some chords here and there, a few bars of the Bach *English Suite* he had been practicing at home, a bit of Scarlatti. He seemed transfixed by each instrument, his ears cocked to their tones, his fingers stroking their ebony carved keys. He bent to examine their painted lids, their elaborate rose holes, he tried their various stops, pulling and pushing devices for changing registers. He had forgotten I was in the room, and how he had tortured me to get here and how I had almost died. I was expendable in order that he have his satisfactions. He played the various instruments for about twenty minutes. Finally, when I could wait no longer, I went down the stairs in search of a bathroom and met the famous man coming back up carrying a small tray with food and wine glasses on it.

"The bathroom?" I asked, and he pointed down the stairs and to the right. I found a tiny room and in it was an ancient toilet, not clean, the seat up. He lived here alone.

❁

The man served us squares of foccacia with green olives buried in the salty bread, and some local red wine. He spoke briefly about his concert schedule, here and in the states. Then he stood up and indicated he was done with us. The visit was over, he had someplace to go. "It was nice to meet you and glad you could stop by." He indicated we should follow him to the door.

"I am not walking down that mountain," I announced.

The man stopped, puzzled. He thought for a moment. "Well, then, perhaps you should call a cab." He waited to see which one of us would pull out a cell phone. Then said, "I guess I'll have to call one for you."

He left the room and didn't return for ten minutes. When he did, he said, with irritation, "There's no cab to be had at this hour. They don't want to drive up here when they have all the fares they need in the center."

"That's too bad," I said, staying seated.

"I'm sorry," my husband said, "to be so much trouble."

The man looked as if he agreed with him—more trouble than he wanted to deal with. "I suppose I'll have to take you down the mountain, then."

❁

We followed him outside to where his sports car was parked. He pointed to another mountain across a valley. "The pianist Andres Schiff lives over there," he said.

"We don't plan to visit him," I said, for my husband's benefit.

The harpsichordist indicated I would have to sit on my husband's lap for the trip down the mountain. He roared onto the road at an extremely high speed, taking hairpin turns like a race car driver. Curve after curve, I braced myself, and fell to one side, then another. Was it possible we had walked up the mountain *this far*?

When we got to the bottom, to Porta Romana, he let us off. I felt he should take us ten minutes further to San Marco, or even to our doorway on Via Ricasole just down the street from Michelangelo's *David*. Since we'd had no dinner, he could have been decent and bought us ice cream at the gelateria, the place where we had hid for safety the last time we almost lost our lives.

But the great man dropped us off at the bus stop in view of the woman carrying her eternal burden and sped away without so much as a wave.

We waited there for the bus to come for a long, long time. The wind was very cold. My husband slumped against the wall and hung his head. He looked old and melancholy. After a while, I leaned backward against his body. I felt I might faint. He turned me around and held my face in his hands. I let my body fall against his, my head on his shoulder. He told me he would hail the first cab he saw.

We waited and waited but none passed by. Then we saw the lights of the bus and he stepped forward and held up his hand.

The Lost Airman: A Memoir of World War Two

O**N THE 6TH OF FEBRUARY,** 1943, my cousin Henry Sherman, the most beautiful soldier I had ever seen, disappeared into thin air over a place called New Guinea. I had expected this news ever since he taught me to sing the song of the Army Air Corps:

"We live in fame, go down in flame,

Nothing can stop the Army Air Corps."

Before this, when he wrote our family from flight school, I had already begun to worry about him. One letter, which my mother read to us, alarmed me:

"Dear Folks, Flew like an angel yesterday. Things are getting tougher. I'm really learning how to twist that plane around the skies . . . I like flying upside down best of all."

It was clear to me, from the times my father had held me upside-down, that Henry would become dizzy and be unable to steer his airplane. After his graduation from flight school, he came home to visit on his last furlough. My grandmother told him she was worried about him going so far away and began to cry a little. Henry took a silver dollar from his pocket and tossed it in the air. "My lucky silver dollar, Gram," he said. "It always lands heads up—see? I scratched my name on it. I'll be just fine."

He let me touch the dollar, then lifted me high on his shoulder while my father took a picture of us. The sun, glinting off the gold pilot's wings on the front of his hat, thrilled me and made me happy. Wherever Henry was, life was exciting. The brim of his hat was stiff, the points of his shirt collar were ruler-straight, and his sleeves had a sharp crease from shoulder to wrist. He gleamed with perfection, whereas my father, who didn't get to fight in the war because of me, because he had a wife and a child, always dressed in baggy pants, his shirt pulled out at the waist. His curly hair was wild and unruly, and sometimes he didn't shave. Because he had an antique shop and worked with old furniture and dusty statues, his fingernails were always grimy.

Sometimes I wished that Henry, who was exactly twenty years older than I was (we shared the same birthday, March 15th), could be my father. He knew what I needed. He promised to send me presents from wherever he landed his plane in the world, from every base, from every far-away city. "I will think of you wherever I go," he told me, kissing my cheek hard with his beautiful lips. "I will send you dolls and fans and little bells and carved peacocks with great colorful tails."

I was almost five and I adored him. Our mothers were sisters, although his mother, my Aunt Eva, was born twelve years before my mother and from a different father than my mother's. She was tall and very magnificent. She wore great white corsets with laces and hooks and had no hesitation in pulling off her dress in front of me if she chose to, making me look at her flesh, the garters with which she held up her stockings, her shimmering large breasts. My own mother was thin and modest. She dressed with her face and half her body in the closet, letting me see only the curve of her bare back. Sometimes she even carried her nightgown into the bathroom to put it on.

The third sister, my Aunt Greta, born two years after my mother, had no husband, no children, and she lived in the house in Brooklyn with my mother, father, grandmother and me because she had no choice and nowhere else to go.

My Aunt Eva lived not in Brooklyn but the Bronx, not in a house with a backyard and a front garden, but in a tall apartment building with a marble foyer and an elevator. Her husband, my Uncle

Eddie, was a prize-fighter and though he was short and very solid, he didn't scare me, even with his broken nose. In addition to Henry, they had two other sons, Irving and Freddy, one older than Henry, one younger. All three were handsome and fun to be with, I was proud to be related to them.

⚜

The war, to a child in Brooklyn in the 1940s, meant several specific things: you were not allowed to interrupt a news broadcast, especially if your father tilted his head toward the radio and held up his hand to stop you from speaking; you were encouraged to make balls out of silver foil from chewing gum wrappers and discarded cigarette packs found in the street, and you were urged to give up any costume jewelry or beads that you had in your jewel box. The tinfoil balls would in some way help our boys win the war, whereas the beads and rings could be traded for food to the wild men of New Guinea should our boys happen to crash-land in the mountains and need to barter with the natives. All children were urged to buy war stamps for 10 cents each, to be pasted in a little book. Eventually, when the book was filled up, a war bond could be purchased. This would also help win the war. Winning the war was what we had to do in order for Henry to come home safe and be with us again. Fighting the war meant that we had to draw black curtains over our windows when the blackout alarm was sounded. Our giving up new leather shoes, eating lamb chops, and sugar to make cakes would mean there was more for the boys to have. It was all quite simple. If we did those things, Hitler would be destroyed and the enemy would be conquered.

❋

After Henry's disappearance, my family waited for news, any kind of news except a telegram. The sight of telegram boys who rode bicycles through our neighborhood to deliver bad news was dreaded by everyone. The fact that Henry had disappeared was bad enough, but everyone in my family and in my house was certain he was alive, which was good. The telegram boys had the power to deliver the worst news of all: that someone's son had been killed and would never come home. Mothers whose sons were killed in the war were given gold stars to paste in their window, just as I (who was in kindergarten) was given gold stars when I knew my numbers or colors or could tell the correct time on the clock in the classroom. My Aunt Eva did not get a gold star for two reasons: one was that Henry was not proven dead, he was only "missing in action"; and two (I assumed) was because she had no window facing on the street on which to paste a gold star. I wondered privately if she would want to move to a one-story house (preferably in Brooklyn, near us) to display her star if the telegram boy ever delivered the worst news of all.

Lost boys were not new to our family. I already had one lost uncle, my mother's older brother, Sam. (Sam and my Aunt Eva were children of my grandmother's first husband, whereas my mother and Aunt Greta came from her second.) My grandmother had a missing son who she was certain was still alive and, now, so did her daughter. My mother had also lost a son shortly after I was born, but he had died by miscarriage so no one was expecting him to return. I imagined that someday I would probably also be required to have a missing son, I did not look forward to it, although I recognized that it brought you a great deal of attention, and visitors, and phone calls and allowed you to go to your room to cry because you were having "a very hard time of it." Everyone in my house did a great deal of crying, my grandmother and my mother and my Aunt

Greta. I also felt I had something to cry about: no dolls, no fans, no peacocks and no bells from foreign countries.

My grandmother, from the time her son was lost (long before I was born), insisted on leaving the front porch lights of the house lit up every night because she continued to expect Sam to come walking in the door. She consulted fortune-tellers as to his whereabouts. She took part in seances. Others in the family presumed he had drowned. He had gone fishing with friends on the eve of Yom Kippur (in a storm, no less), a very bad time to have an outing since (as my Aunt Greta explained to me) that was the night all Jews were required to begin 24 hours of fasting—not even drinking water—to atone for their sins. Sam should have been in shul, praying to God. She blamed Sam's bad lot of friends for enticing him to go fishing that night, boys who didn't have any respect for their families or their upbringing.

I could understand the lure of fishing. My father often took me fishing, in a rowboat in Prospect Park or on a pier at Sheepshead Bay, but we never went at night. It seemed there would be no point in going at night. How then could we see the sunshine on the water, the silvery dance of the fish on the line, the desperate struggle of its flapping fins on the wood floor of the boat or the pier, the heaving of its gills as it tried to breathe in air, and its final scaly stillness after it gasped a last time and gave up the fight?

My mother had told me that after her brother had drowned on that stormy Yom Kippur night, she—though she was only seventeen—had been called many times to the morgue to look at the faces of drowned men in case one of them might be Sam. My grandmother could not be asked to do it, nor could Aunt Greta. When I begged my mother to describe what dead men looked like, she refused to tell me, but she assured me that though she sometimes wished one of them had been Sam so the family could have gotten the thousand dollar insurance policy which would have paid the mortgage on the house, she was also glad not one of them had ever turned out to be Sam.

Between my grandmother still thinking Sam would come marching in the door, and my Aunt Eva certain Henry would hike out of the mountains in New Guinea and phone her from somewhere, I felt thankful my father came from a family of no missing sons and had no expectations that ghosts would appear at the door. Now and then he threatened to join up and fight in the war because he felt useless not being "over there"—but my mother and I begged him to remember how much we needed him over here.

In the weeks following Henry's disappearance, my Aunt Eva came over many Friday nights with her boys (really, they were men), Freddy and Irving, to share my grandmother's boiled chicken and kreplach soup at our house. (Uncle Eddie still played poker with his cronies on Friday nights, though Aunt Eva said he had gone to pieces since Henry was missing and would never be the same.) After dinner, as soon as we all got to talking about how likely it was that Henry would still return, Aunt Eva would take the letter from her purse, written by Henry's commanding officer, and read it again to us to prove that there was still hope:

Dear Mrs. Sherman:

How it pains me to write you this, the saddest duty of my life. Your son was a fine young man, a good friend of mine. I knew of his devotion to you . . . All I can do now is tell you what we know happened on the 6th day of February, 1943. On that day we took a flight of our ships to Uau, New Guinea. Six in all. Over the Uau airport we were attacked by about forty Zeros and some Bombers. Henry was flying a ship called "Early Delivery" with Lt. R. H. Schwensen, Cpl. Erickson, Private Faun and Private Piekutowski. The Zeros came in fast and four were diving at Henry's ship. He went near the port in a turn and from then on—no one is sure. It's not anything to help your feelings, but the Japs lost 26 in this fight to (I am sorry to say) our one. In this land of thousands of miles of jungles, mountains, and God knows what, anything is possible. But all we can do is look and try to find his ship . . . As long as we are in New Guinea— we'll be looking.

These letters are harder to write than the war—Henry was my friend and Buddy—and if there is any way to find him, we will do it. You can rest assured in that.
Yours sincerely,
Robert. L. Ward, Captain, 33rd Troop Carrier Squadron.

Through the War Department, Aunt Eva had managed to get in touch with the Schwensens, the parents of Henry's co-pilot, who lived in Wichita, Kansas and now the two mothers began to write to each other very often. Aunt Eva read us Mrs. Schwensen's letters, too:

Dear Mr. and Mrs. Sherman:

I know it will help you out to know there is someone else who had a son on Robert's plane beside us—her husband is a lieutenant in New Guinea. He talked to a native down there and the native said he knew where Robert's plane was and so they have sent a group of natives to map out a way for the investigators to get in, as the area is very remote and the jungle there is very dense. Her husband said at the time of their flight, they were carrying food as cargo, so if the boys weren't hurt, they'd be able to exist quite a while on the food which was aboard. He also said that they don't think the boys are prisoners of the Japanese because of the remoteness of the area where the plane went down. I am glad you have so much faith and courage, because I really think that—in itself— will help the boys wherever they are. This gives all of us added hope that the boys will ultimately be reached by this rescue group and trust by now that we will hear something definite and that they are all well. Should we hear further shortly we will give you the information providing you do not hear before we do, with best wishes we are,
The Schwensens.

"So anything is still possible," said my Aunt Greta.

"Anything is possible," agreed my mother. "And if there is any way to find him, they will."

"I know he'll come back," I added, though I was not sure at all.

It was that same night my cousin Freddy announced to Aunt Eva: "Ma, I went downtown today and enlisted. I'm going to train as a navigator. I told them I want to be sent to the Pacific. I'm going to get the bastards that got my brother."

"Oh please!" Aunt Eva cried. "Don't do that to me."

"I've done it, Ma. Please don't cry. You know I have to go. You don't really want to stop me, do you?"

✿

By August of 1943, when Freddy had been shipped out to the European theater with the 82nd Airborne, my Aunt Eva got another letter from Mrs. Schwensen:

Dear Mr. and Mrs. Sherman:

On July 5, Jimmie Campbell, who is now a captain, and who had been in the South Pacific area for nearly fifteen months, returned home from New Guinea. He was the leader of the flight on February 6th when Robert's and Henry's transport was apparently lost. He came to our home and talked to us a long time. He does paint a very dark picture for us as to the boys' safety. Of course, he was also giving us the Government's viewpoint as to their being lost and, as you already know, the Government does not hold much hope for the boys' safety. Nevertheless, they also do not have sufficient proof. The boys could still be safe because the plane has not been found. He explained all matters in detail as to how it happened that fateful day. He said they all really expected to be shot down when the enemy appeared on the scene that day. Anti-aircraft fire from our ground forces and fighter planes shot down twenty-eight Zeros out of about thirty-eight that day; but two Zeros broke through somehow and pounced on our boys' plane and, apparently, they were the victims.

We want to quote to you from a letter from our eldest son, who is training in this country as a pilot, as follows: 'I have thought over and over again many times the conversation Robert and I had in San Antonio, when he said that he knew just what to do in case he was face to face with a situation . . . he said he would use his demolition equipment to destroy his plane after everybody had taken to the parachutes. This is the reason they haven't found his plane. It had secret radar equipment which he swore to destroy before crashing. He had rehearsed this action over so many times in his mind that it was just part of him. I just now that he is alive somewhere.'

So you see we have not given up hope as yet and we do not want you to either. Still trusting and hoping for the safe return of all our boys missing. With best wishes we are, Bess and Justus Schwensen.

※

Freddy sent me an embroidered silk blouse from Belgium with a matching skirt whose bodice laced up high at the waist, and a china doll I named Alice, for whom my Aunt Greta made a head of hair out of black wool. I could braid this hair, though it wasn't as good as the blonde hair on the heads of certain dolls my friends had, the sort of doll that cost too much for my parents to buy for me.

Aunt Greta joined the Red Cross and spent days at the synagogue, making bandages out of gauze and knitting socks for the boys overseas. I often went with her, sitting at long tables with other women who rolled gauze and knitted socks. If there were sheets of loose tinfoil that had been brought in, I was given the job of adding them to the growing silver ball whose purpose in the war effort I didn't exactly understand, though a silver ball, as big as a basketball, was an impressive thing to see. My mother had begun to save the grease from cooked bacon in a tin can, although we were Jewish and were not supposed to eat bacon. My father hated the smell of it; my mother said the grease oiled the tanks and therefore she intended to cook it every day, her contribution to winning the war.

When my cousin Freddy's plane was shot at over France, he got an arm and a leg full of shrapnel and had to be shipped home to a hospital in the USA. My Aunt Eva cried tears of joy, and seemed oddly happy that her son's leg was infected and full of holes. When they cut out the seventy-seven little pieces of metal, she put them in a velvet case in her jewel box. She also had in her jewel box Henry's medals, conferred upon him by the War Department, the Distinguished Flying Cross and the Purple Heart. Whenever we went to visit her in the Bronx, she let me hold the medals. which were cold, brown and hard, and didn't seem like much of a present if you were never going to come home again.

The war was lasting so long it was making everyone crazy. Every time we went shopping and passed the house of Mrs. Carp on East Fourth Street, we stopped to witness the four gold stars in her front window. Aunt Greta always said to my mother, "My God, My God, how does she keep living?" And then we had to do the ordinary things, walk on to the bakery and the butcher and the drugstore.

Suddenly though, when no one expected the war would ever end, the war ended. People rushed into the street, screaming and tossing confetti in the air. Strangers lifted me into the air and kissed me. I never saw so much love in my life. I felt proud that my work on the silver foil balls must have had something to do with all this happiness.

❋

In November of 1945, a neighbor told my Aunt Greta that an article had appeared in *The New York News* on November 12th titled "Lindy Over Shangri-La"—reporting that Charles Lindbergh had discovered some American planes on a mountain top in New Guinea. Aunt Greta wrote at once to the newspaper to ask if they would send her the article. The head of the Information Bureau responded quickly: "We regret to say that our supply of copies of that paper has been depleted. According to that article, however, Charles Lindbergh flew low over an isolated spot in the New Guinea jungle and discovered a primitive valley in Dutch New Guinea. There he saw three C-47 transports, an A-20 attack bomber, a Douglas dive bomber and two British planes which had made emergency landings and had been stranded because they could not take off in the rarefied air on a short runway. You may address Mr. Lindbergh in care of the Ford Motor Company, Detroit, Michigan."

My aunt wrote at once to Lindbergh and begged him to reply, to reveal, if he only could, that perhaps—by some great good fortune—her nephew was a survivor of one of those forced landings.

She watched out the window for the mailman every day. While she wished for mail, she prayed that the telegram boy would never stop anywhere on our block. She told me that Lindbergh, a brave man and famous flier, had also lost a son a long time ago, a baby boy who was stolen from his crib by a murderer. She knew that if the letter got to him, he would answer it. She knew he would understand what our family's pain was like.

When the letter came two weeks later, my aunt opened it as if she were unwrapping a precious jewel. She read us every word:

The Tompkins House
Long Lots Road
Westport, Conn.

December 4, 1945

Miss Greta Sorblum
405 Avenue "O"
Brooklyn 30
New York, New York

Dear Miss Sorblum:

I am extremely sorry to have to tell you in reply to your letter, that the newspaper report about my seeing an isolated place in New Guinea, cut off from communications, where several planes had made forced landings is untrue as are so many similar stories printed these days.

I want you to know that you have my deepest sympathy in your great concern for your nephew who has been reported missing. I wish I had information which might be of value to you.
    Sincerely,
    Charles Lindbergh

❄

In 1985, when I was a grown woman with children of my own, I traveled to Miami Beach from California to attend my 30th high school reunion. Aunt Eva was living then in a retirement hotel for the very old a block from the beach. She had lost the voluptuous flesh that had made her seem bigger than life when I was a little girl, and now appeared to me as if she had slowly vanished over the years. She lived in one room in a decrepit 1920s' hotel on Collins Avenue that offered an ocean view. She was waiting on the front porch for me and the minute we got to her room, she pressed upon me everything she could think of that was hers to give: an old slice of French toast wrapped in tinfoil that she was planning to reheat in the toaster, a little china lamb that sat on top of her television, a nylon sweater beaded with pearls that she thought would look good on me at the formal dinner I was to attend that evening and she insisted I eat a big round cookie that she had been saving in her tiny refrigerator, the kind we used to call as kids "black and whites." Her husband and her oldest son, Irving, were long dead, my grandmother and my father were dead, her son Freddy, a successful investment broker, lived two thousand miles away.

When we began to talk of Henry, she told me that his best buddy had married Henry's girlfriend; together they'd had three children. "Everyone is gone. Uncle Eddie. Irving. Sam. My mother and my father. It's all like a dream."

"I always thought it so strange that Sam and Henry were both lost," I said. "Two boys in one family."

"Sam wasn't lost. He was killed."

"He was killed? I thought he drowned in a fishing accident."

"No. Sam and his friends weren't going fishing that night. They were running rum up and down the coast. They were making a lot of money at it. Sam always had an eye for the quick buck. There was a rival boat that was stealing their business. They fired on each other. The Coast Guard got involved, who knows. Both boats were shot down. They both sank. No one survived."

"Grandma always thought he would still come home."

"We all think what we have to think," Aunt Eva said.

❖

Before I left, my aunt and I looked through some old photos and came upon the one of Henry holding me on his shoulder at his last furlough: I'm four years old, wearing a sweater and overalls and a knit hat with a pompom on it. My small hand is wrapped around the back of Henry's neck, and he—in his starched uniform, his Air Corps hat with his pilot's wings above the brim—shines resplendent.

Aunt Eva said, "I want you to have Henry's things—his letters from flight school, the picture album he sent me that shows him posing with all his airplanes and his buddies, the letter from his commander after he was lost, the letters from the Schwensens. Take good care of them. Tell your children so they know what happened. Tell them war is no good."

❖

In 1989, a little more than a year after my Aunt Eva died at the age of 92, my husband and I were having coffee and browsing through the Los Angeles Times when a back-page article caught my eye:

Airman Buried 46 Years After Death in Jungle

Leavenworth, Kansas—Nearly half a century ago, a young Army airman left his wife and family in Wichita to fight in World War II over the Pacific Ocean. On Friday, 1st Lt. Robert Schwensen was finally laid to rest here, a year after his remains were discovered by Australian gold prospectors atop a mountain in a dense jungle of New Guinea. Schwensen and four other men aboard a C-47 had been listed as missing in action since their aircraft was shot down by Japanese fighter planes in February, 1943. Schwensen was buried Friday under overcast skies with an honor guard and a 21-gun salute at Ft. Leavenworth's National Cemetery. "At last he's going to finally be home where he belongs," said June Rockhill, the woman Robert Schwensen left behind in the fall of 1942. She was 18 at the time and had been married just three months . . . Air Force officials in Washington said it is rare to find the remains of missing servicemen so long after World War II.

"Robert Schwensen!" I cried out. "Oh my God! I've got to call my cousin Freddy."

❖

Freddy immediately called the Department of War and learned that Henry's skeletal remains had been found in the pilot's seat on the left side of the transport plane's cockpit, his dog-tags still around his bones, with his belt, his knife, his eye-glass frames and his lucky silver dollar lying nearby. Robert Schwensen's body was also in the cockpit, on the right side. The bones of the other three airmen were intermingled in the back compartment of the plane. The government had been unable to locate any of the missing boys' families so long after the war, although when news of the plane's discovery was printed in a newspaper, a relative of the Schwensen family living in Del Mar, California, saw it and called the government for more information. Finally, the family was able to claim the body of their boy.

Freddy called me back the next day—hardly able to suppress the tears in his voice—to report that Henry would now be buried, with full military honors, in Arlington National Cemetery. The government was sending him Henry's lucky silver dollar and the few other personal effects that had survived the ravages of the years. Freddy said he was glad his mother hadn't lived to hear the news. "To know that they found my brother would have killed her."

✿

After much searching through the phone book and making calls, I managed to find the address of E.W. "Swede" Schwensen, Robert Schwensen's brother, and sent him news that we were part of Henry's family, and that we, too, had discovered our boy's remains. He wrote me back at once: "We just returned this week from Ft. Leavenworth National cemetery where Lt. Robt H. Schwensen was buried six plots from his older brother Capt. Justus Schwensen, a B-24 pilot killed over Hamburg, Germany. Our family also lost a third brother, Lt. Richard Schwensen (Infantry) killed at Remagen Bridge in Germany and is buried in the American Cemetery in Luxembourg. Mother and Dad are deceased, but my younger brother and myself attended Robert's funeral . . . It's nice to have all this behind us now so that we can go on with our lives."

A three-star family, I thought to myself. How did they bear it?

I didn't go to Henry's funeral, but one day when my grown daughters were in the garage looking through some of their old childhood toys, they unearthed a box of gold paper stars. I took one of them and pressed it in the corner of my bedroom window—my small salute to Henry, the most beautiful soldier I had ever known.

On the Edge of the Action:
A Conversation With Merrill Joan
Gerber by Mario Materassi

This interview took place in the office of Mario Materassi, Professor of American Literature at the University of Florence, in Florence, Italy in the fall of 1996.

MARIO MATERASSI Let's begin from the very beginning. When did you start writing?

MERRILL JOAN GERBER For sure, at age seven. My aunt had a beauty shop and I started writing little poems about her customers, you know, "My aunt has a customer Sadie/She is a nice lady." I had a desire to use words and describe what I knew, to record the inner and outer observances of my life as if they were important. When I was at an early age, my father got me a typewriter. I took it down to the basement, and I remember thinking to myself, I'm now alone, away from the tumult of the household, and now I will write to someone who really understands. Someone who was sensitive, alert, intelligent, all the things that the relatives and the parents were not.

MATERASSI Or you thought they were not.

GERBER I know for a fact: none of them was the perfect reader. We were living in Brooklyn at that time, my mother and father downstairs, my unmarried aunt upstairs with my grandmother. And I, as the only child before my sister was born, was the point of battle between my aunt and my mother. My aunt wanted me and my mother wanted me, and they both told me how awful the other was—and why what she wanted for me was wrong. My aunt wanted to teach me how to bake and cook and sew. My mother had contempt for those household joys, and she wanted to teach me rhyming and Beethoven and what little culture she had. She didn't have very much culture, but she had a great desire to be a cultured American, whereas my aunt had a great wish to make me aware of my Jewish background.

MATERASSI So it appears that your mother won.

GERBER No. My mother had very little interest in the personal nature of each person's growth, even her own. But my aunt was always looking at the tiny details of everyone's life, and she gave me a sense that it was important: what someone said, who didn't marry who, who committed suicide and why. So I don't think the mother triumphed.

MATERASSI You did become an intellectual and a writer, however, which is something that your mother was more interested in than your aunt was.

GERBER Right. And my aunt continues to think that it's a worthless achievement. She often tells me about other people she knows who have really good jobs such as a bookkeeper or as a storekeeper or even someone who owns a print shop. And then she says to me of my daughters, who are all in graduate school: "When are they going to do something useful?"

MATERASSI And what about your father?

GERBER He was the philosopher of the household. He had a very brief education, but he loved to read. He took me out to Prospect Park, and he would say, "Look at the beautiful lake, look at the sun.

The best things in life are free." He loved food, he loved nature, he loved animals: he had that kind of warmth. So among the aunt, the mother, and the father, I had three parents. I sensed (although this is in retrospect) that each gave me the germ of the writer that comes together in me: the long view, the petty attention to detail, and the wish for language and literature. I owe a lot to all of them.

MATERASSI When did you decide that you would write as a way of being?

GERBER When I got to college and began seeing the literary quarterlies in the library. I had already been writing stories that I sent away to magazines from age thirteen on, and so I knew that it was possible to write. But, when I saw that it could be a way of life, that other people had the same kind of vision that I had, that stories in these journals echoed some of my perceptions of life, I thought, I will be this! I will read Thomas Wolfe and I will be as great as he! I just knew that this was what I wanted to do, and also that it was the only arena in which I could be honest to myself and to what I understood to be the truth about life. Because in social circumstances one had always to be deceitful, polite, politically correct. Maybe not then, but now. One never told the truth. In polite society we just talk on the surface, and I couldn't live on that surface. So I had to go home and write what I felt and what I saw. I don't know how that nature develops in any writer. I don't have any writers in my family. I had books. I had many books. My father, who was an antiques dealer, would bring home these cartons of books, and I considered them mine. And there I was, with all sorts of books, none of which had any connection to my age or life. But I learned what life was about from those books. Life in Brooklyn was not all of life, and that was a surprise to me. But, if you read a book, you could go to England; you could have a lover; you could have a baby. Even *Gone with the Wind* was a great thing to read at thirteen.

MATERASSI You did not have a formal Jewish upbringing, did you?

GERBER Not really. On the High Holy Days my father went to shul, with my aunt. My mother had no use for that. My mother liked to trick my father who did not want to eat, say, milk and meat. When she made lamb chops and mashed potatoes, she sometimes put butter in the potatoes. My father would eat dinner, and she'd say to him, "Hah! You didn't even know there was butter in the potatoes!"

MATERASSI How did he take it?

GERBER I think he was upset. But he loved my mother, or he was afraid of her, and he tolerated a lot of abuse from her. The few times that he hit me, it was to quiet her in her rage against me. I was such a bad child because I didn't finish my food, and she was going to take iodine and kill herself, and how could I be such a bad child? And my father, occasionally, would hit me but almost with a signal to me that this is really not for you; this is to show her that I understand how bad you are. But we know you are not a bad child.

MATERASSI Did it work?

GERBER Usually. Sometimes she stormed out of the house. She was a great histrionic actress. Sometimes I feel that kind of thing coming over me, the wish to make a scene, which I hate in myself. I think she felt a tremendous frustration. She was a talented pianist. She worked for two state senators in New York as a legal secretary from a very early age, and they recognized her intelligence and offered to send her to law school at their expense, but at night, so that she could work for them in the day. She didn't have the strength to work all day, go to school, and study all night. So I think all her life she felt that she had married beneath her. She married an uneducated man, whereas she could have married a lawyer or a doctor or whoever came into those offices. She was an angry woman all her working life and has very little sweetness or kindness in her. I think

I am a kinder person than she is, but I also know I have that edge of infantile tendency to rage. We all have those sides that we wouldn't like to be seen in public. But I think that the writer is often self-analytical and recognizes the things that are not admirable, and maybe where they come from. The writer is full of self-analysis, as well as excessive analysis of everything he or she sees and does.

MATERASSI Some time ago you said that you feel you have missed out on the fun in life.

GERBER I think the essence of the writer is always to be on the edge of the action and to observe. A writer spends a lot of time mulling, not dancing, not partying, not drinking. And maybe wishing to be free of this analytical mode.

MATERASSI One of your stories, "Tabu," seems to be a paradigm of the artist's point of view.

GERBER That's the perfect sense of myself as a child: watching, thinking, wishing, wanting to be the beautiful, popular star of the kissing game, the one who gives the party and who relishes it, not the one who barely gets to it and then can't enjoy it once she gets there. It's a mixed blessing.

At times I have felt that it is the greatest thing in the world to have this gift, understanding life as far as I can understand it. At other times I think, "Look at all the people who don't seem to think much at all: are they having less pain, more fun? How can we ever know what anybody else's life is like?"

MATERASSI In your writing, you seem to be more interested in the inter play between people than in the relationship between people and their physical or political environment.

GERBER When I was young and reading novels, I was so bored by the first three pages which described the town nestled at the edge of the valley and the river, and I'd think, Let's get to where the people are. I was also being raised in a very urban environment where nobody knew the name of a tree. Who needed to know the names? I knew we had a lilac tree in the front yard and a peach tree in the back yard. But, in terms of visual appreciation of the world, I got none as a child except my father saying the ocean is pretty. We didn't look at art. The objects in my father's shop were just for commerce. He once bought an oil painting by Frederic Remington; I think he paid a hundred dollars for it, and he sold it immediately for two hundred. My mother occasionally did research so she'd know if a signed thing was real. But no one ever said, look at art, look at nature. We were all in the house. It was cold, it was winter, we were inside. So it's true that there is a dearth of external description in my work.

MATERASSI But it wasn't always winter. There must have been summers, too.

GERBER Oh, in the summer, there was polio. You couldn't go out, you couldn't drink from the fountain, you couldn't go to the park. We didn't go to the beach, you could drown at the beach. You couldn't go on the sand, you could get sunburned. We had a lot of fear of death in our house. One of my relatives was shot down during World War II; my mother's brother was lost at sea when he was twenty-five; my grandfather died in his forties. Before my father came home late at night, after going on calls to buy antiques, the women in the house would say, "Maybe someone killed him." And we'd look out of the window to see if he'd ever come home.

MATERASSI I remember this scene in *The Kingdom of Brooklyn*.

GERBER That's right. I didn't realize until years later that not every family feared that death would strike at any second. Fear is at the core of a lot of my sense of being. I would like to rid myself of it at some point, but it hasn't disappeared yet.

MATERASSI Like your fear of Italy.

GERBER That's right! That's the next book? Fear of Italy. I was very afraid to come here. I don't know what I thought would happen, but fear of discomfort, fear of dislocation fear of separation, fear of not having my own down comforter—whatever it might have been.

MATERASSI What is your perception of Jewish American literature? Do you feel a part of it?

GERBER I feared for a long time that I was not a part of it at all because I felt that those who were writing about it had more Jewish education, had more birthright to it, belonged to it more fiercely than I. I also felt that by the time I came to it, it had been well covered by my forebears? Saul Bellow, Philip Roth, Bernard Malamud . . . I felt, What can I add? They have such strong voices and they are so famous by now, and I have this weak little space that I understand which isn't as big a motor turning as the motor they are turning. I was also writing for a middle American magazine in the sixties and seventies, for Redbook. They had me take out all ethnic references. It wasn't until later that I realized that I am a Jewish writer, I lived in a Jewish family, I am as Jewish as anybody. I may not be religious and I may not be Orthodox, but I understand the Jewish psyche, and I have one. And it's my right to claim my space. I realized that I had my foot in a special and unusual place: I had spent my life growing up between my aunt and my mother; now they were both old ladies; they both called me many times a day with their stories of their angers, their miseries, the way they were mistreated. And I took their voices to be my own. That's when I began writing the stories about Anna, the old Jewish woman, and a few other things that directly reflected that fact that I have a Jewish mentality and psyche and that my dreams are Jewish. I feel I have as strong a Jewish voice as anybody, although Cynthia Ozick, my dear, dear friend, might say, or did say when she reviewed my first book many years ago, that the only thing Jewish about my work was the smell of the delicatessen in my stories. She has since retracted those unkind words, but from time to time she has to castigate me for not being Jewish enough. But I am what I am, as Popeye says; and I do see myself as coming at the tail end of a great Jewish renaissance. Now I see a different kind of renaissance in American literature, a great deal of attention being paid to South American and Asian and African-American writers, which is fair enough. But I think that my little flag of being a Jewish writer is not so interesting anymore. It may be over for Jewish writers.

MATERASSI Are you talking about a question of market or about the watering down of Jewishness because of assimilation?

GERBER I think both. The publishing market has an eye toward what it's looking for, and Jewish life is just not as interesting as it was: the Jews have come, made their place, their children are doctors and lawyers, their grandchildren are already throwing it off and intermarrying and forgetting about being Jewish. I am one of those people, too, who has a mixed feeling: did I educate my children in a Jewish way or a Jewish-enough way? Certainly, emotionally, yes. Certainly, with the humor and history of our family, yes. But formal religion is hard for me to take. As soon as I get into a place where they start raising money by bingo games and Las Vegas games for the shul, I have to leave. I don't have the patience for that kind of community, although I understand those places need to be supported. But, if I am to go, I want a rabbi who is a poet and a genius and a literary person.

MATERASSI You want Chaim Potok.

GERBER I want Moses!

MATERASSI Excuse me.

GERBER I just want to be able to listen to someone with wisdom. If I go to sit in a space where I'm going to be talked at and told to think and meditate on the meaning of my life, I always want to say, "But I do that all the time. I don't just do that on Friday night." Maybe I'm the rabbi.

MATERASSI Reformed?

GERBER Definitely Reformed!

MATERASSI My next questions concern your craft, how you came to it, how you developed it, how it reflects your vision of the world.

GERBER Among the things that I think are essential are a voice, and a point of view that is singular. Each of us has a vision of life. We cannot have an omniscient vision. As I was growing up and becoming a more critical reader, I could see that a novel that had multiple points of view, or an omniscient point of view in which you are in everybody's head at once, just confused me. I wanted to enter the psyche of a character and experience everything through that character. It seemed to me the best way to work. So I chose that as one of the things I would always do in my work: be in the mind of a person and let him or her observe and react, rather than imagine what other people are thinking. The other thing I decided was never to use my imagination to invent the impossible. A lot of writers take the vocabulary of television or the movies or other books to be their own vocabulary. I think that to write well you need to have your own vocabulary. You need to have been there, seen it, done it, felt it, thought it yourself. Although writers are supposed to have great imaginations, I think I have an imagination that is limited to a leap from here (what I know) to there (what I can imagine). It doesn't leapfrog, miles away, to a soldier on the battlefield or to a prostitute. So I suppose I have limited myself to be as truthful as I can. I think the strongest thing in writing is a kind of honesty and vision, not imaginary acts of imaginary people. This is both a limitation and a strength because you can't write War and Peace if you can't imagine lives far and away from your own, and I haven't written *War and Peace*, not yet. Those writers of genius who can do that, and do it well, are amazing. But a lot of current writers don't do it well and don't create real human beings.

MATERASSI But, when you read, you don't necessarily know whether or not the writer writes out of a personal experience. With a good writer you should not be able to tell the difference.

GERBER Right. When I read the works of Flannery O'Connor I felt the truth of her characters. Though she might not have been the girl without the leg, she could understand the girl without the leg who is seduced by the Bible salesman. She even says that you must be able to leap from the thing that happened to what could have happened. That can be a great imaginative leap. But it has to stay within a certain possibility of what the character is capable of. But I don't think a whole lot about technique, style, craft, or the way I write. It's a kind of instinctive thing. I don't know the language of the newest criticism. I have no knowledge of what they are doing in literary criticism.

MATERASSI You once studied it, didn't you?

GERBER Yes. I studied with Andrew Lytle and Wallace Stegner. But they were both interested in a kind of craft that didn't have fancy critical words attached. There were some very simple things that Lytle taught us. Point of view was one, and enveloping action was another, and action proper was another.

MATERASSI What did he mean by enveloping action?

GERBER The world in which the story takes place, whether it's during a war or a depression, the context. The action proper is what happens among people. So they are very simple terms. I don't spend much time being a critic or reading other critics. I just do my work, and I know when I am in the space of the right voice and the right rhythm.

MATERASSI I hope it's clear that I am not accusing you of not reading criticism or not using critical jargon. What I am interested in is your view of the "leap" concept. Because the leap between what happened and what could have happened might still reach over an enormous distance. Certainly, the possibility of going from A to B has to be inherent in the character, but it appears to me that you are talking about a leap that concerns your imagination rather than the character's.

GERBER Yes. That's very true. My novel *King of the World* has a character in it who is a disturbed man, maybe mentally ill, psychotic, paranoid. This character always felt to himself: I am not really appreciated enough. I wanted to have this job and I lost it, I have this brilliant idea and nobody appreciates it. This attitude was in the character. But it also reverberated in me as the writer who has good ideas which aren't appreciated or wants approval and doesn't get it. The rejected writer in me, and in all writers, usually has a very strong pull on the mind. And so when I tried to write about this man in his illness, in his insanity, in his violence, I felt some of that coming from some place in me as the writer who is enraged, who is rejected, who is ignored, who didn't make it. I think he is one of my great characters, although he is as far from a little Jewish girl in Brooklyn as could possibly be. That was a big leap for me because he uses obscenities, he is sexually deviant, he is a criminal; he does a lot of things that are far from my experience. But I was his soulmate while I was writing that.

MATERASSI This is what Cynthia Ozick means when she says, "When I write I am not a Jew because in order to write I have to kill."

GERBER Yes, indeed! And that's the other question about being a writer. My family has resisted and rejected my work. Some of my family, not my mother. My mother has always said, "I am proud of you. You do whatever you like." My husband has said, "I won't even read your work if it makes you uncomfortable. I don't want to limit you." My children have stopped telling me things because they want to save their own experiences for their own lives and work: it is dangerous to tell anything to a writer. But some relatives have literally said, "I want nothing more to do with you." They are not readers. They don't understand the tradition and where writers write from. I have even said to some of these people, "As your sister, as your mother, as your daughter, I will be as good a girl as you want me to. I will take care of you, I will fight for you, I will do anything for you. And I love you. But when I am at my desk, I need the freedom not to feel I have to be careful not to step on anybody's toes. It's fiction. What I am doing is fiction. This isn't you. This character has fifty dimensions more than you have. It may look a little like you, and it may be overweight a little like you, but it's not you." I don't think anyone has ever understood that. My daughters do. They all have literary educations. But my older relatives don't. They would like to be proud of me, but they would be a lot prouder if I were selling romance novels and making a lot of money and my books were on every drugstore counter. I had an agent once who said to me, "Put a little more sunshine in your typewriter, and then maybe I can sell your work." That angered me tremendously because my agent should have appreciated that it was pain that drove me, not sunshine. Sunshine is for somebody else. Recently an American woman said to me before I gave a talk here in Florence, "These women are tired, they've worked all day, they want a laugh or two. Please come in and entertain them." Well, they did laugh, and they laughed about the right things. They laughed about the story I told them which was my first sale to a national magazine. It was about the time I had my first child and my mother came to visit me, and what a difficult experience that was. They recognized that they had had the same kind of experience in their own lives. So pain can be a source of laughter.

MATERASSI Probably they laughed also because of the way you told the story. People laugh about language too, not only about situation.

GERBER Yes. I've been telling things about my experience in Italy in little letters home. I just had a letter from Cynthia saying, "Such life you create in such small matters." From her that's a compliment. But to her I write in a much greater arc of freedom of expression than I would to a neighbor.

MATERASSI Well, she certainly knows the difference between the individual and the writer.

GERBER She is the ideal reader, the person you want at the other end of your page. I have a friend who once said, "I don't need to publish books for millions. There are about five people I would like to send my manuscripts to."

MATERASSI Your friend is pretty ambitious. That's almost twice as many as James Joyce had.

GERBER Right. But that's all you want: someone who says, "I know. This is the way it is."

MATERASSI Let me ask you one final question. Is it true that you are less interested in fiction now?

GERBER Yes, I have experienced this change in myself. For years and years I wanted to start a story the next morning, put imaginary words in the minds of imaginary people. And suddenly, that wish to make believe has just fallen away from me. I feel that now I am older, that I have a lot to say from my own mouth, that making up characters doesn't seem doesn't seem to be to be as satisfying to me now. Maybe I am being fed less information. As you age, you withdraw from the world that you have been active in, when you were in school, when you were a young mother, when you were in the world, circulating, which you have to be when you are young because you are building a life. As I get older, I am more encapsulated in my walls, in my mind, in my books, and really understand less of current life than I used to. I am no longer among women who are dating or divorcing. Everybody I know has settled into his or her space now. So I'm not getting the sort of feedback from experience that I used to. And I also have much more time to see the long view and make my own judgments as a person in my own right. I do want to write this book about Italy. It won't be about Italian art, and it won't be about the language, but it will be about a person's intimate vision of Italy for three months of her life. I am interested in doing it, and excited, although a part of me says, "No one will ever want to read this." That's the response I get from the world right now. I feel the world has pretty much withdrawn from wanting to know what I know about it, and that's why I will write what I please now. If it pleases me to write memoirs, like my last book, *Old Mother, Little Cat*, I will do it. Or about my own three months in Italy. My voice is stronger now than any of my characters' voices would be at the present time. This is a whole new experience for me. So this is my answer to your question: I don't know if I will return to fiction.

Merrill Joan Gerber has written thirty books, including *The Kingdom of Brooklyn*, winner of the Ribalow Award from *Hadassah Magazine*, and *King of the World*, winner of the Pushcart Editors' Book Award. Her fiction has been published in the *New Yorker*, the *Sewanee Review*, the *Atlantic*, *Mademoiselle*, and *Redbook*, and her essays in the *American Scholar*, *Salmagundi*, and *Commentary*. She has won an O. Henry Award, a Best American Essays award, and a Wallace Stegner fiction fellowship to Stanford University. She retired in 2020 after teaching writing at the California Institute of Technology for thirty-two years. Her literary archive is now at the Yale Beinecke Rare Book Library.

Printed in the USA
CPSIA information can be obtained
at www.ICGtesting.com
LVHW040930091123
763185LV00040B/383